From the Footplate:

EUROSTAR

From the Footplate:
EUROSTAR

Peter Waller

Ian ALLAN
Publishing

First published 1998

ISBN 0 7110 2427 8

Published by Ian Allan Publishing

an imprint of Ian Allan Publishing Ltd, Terminal House, Station Approach, Shepperton, Surrey TW17 8AS. Printed by Ian Allan Printing Ltd, Riverdene Business Park, Molesey Road, Hersham, Surrey KT12 4RG.

Code: 9808/B2

Front cover: The streamlined nose of the Eurostar power car is perfectly formed for maximum speed.

Back cover, top: The 08.07 Paris Gare du Nord-Waterloo International service passes through Herne Hill station on 5 March 1995. *Brian Morrison*

Back cover, bottom: On 22 January 1995 the 08.07 Paris Gare du Nord-Waterloo International service approaches its destination; the length of the Eurostar train in comparison with the domestic services using Waterloo is evident. *Brian Morrison*

Half title: The driver's-eye view: the French high-speed line — LGV-Nord — stretches out into the distance as the TMST set travels at 300km/h on the approaches to Lille. Note the TVM430 windows directly above the ribbon speedometer. *Colin J. Marsden*

Title page: French-owned TMST Nos 3212/3211 passes Gavrelle on the LGV-Nord on 12 July 1996 *en route* from Waterloo to Paris Gare du Nord with the 16.23 service. *Chris Wilson*

Top: On 16 November 1995 Eurostar sets Nos 3214 and 3205 stand side-by-side at the platform end of Paris Gare du Nord station. The former had just arrived with the 10.23 service from Waterloo. The train shed of Gare du Nord can be seen in the background. Although there were no platform canopies at this time to offer protection to those travelling in coaches furthest from the concourse, SNCF was in the process of constructing them. *Colin J. Marsden*

Above: SNCB-owned TMST sets Nos 3103 and 3104 cross over the high-speed junction at Croiselles with the 13.04 service from Paris to Waterloo on 11 July 1996. *Colin J. Marsden*

Contents

Acknowledgements

As with all books, this project would not have been possible without the assistance of a number of individuals. I would like, in particular, to thank the following: Brian Morrison, Colin J. Marsden, Paul Shannon, Alan Reekie and Simon Pielow. The line drawings on pages 42, 52, 59, 72 and 77 are based on those published by the Quail Map Company in *Railway Track Diagrams 5: England South and London Underground* and I would like to thank John Yonge for granting permission and Gerald Jacobs for providing updated information.

Abbreviations

EPS   European Passenger Services (now Eurostar [UK] Ltd owned by London & Continental)

IECC   Integrated Electronic Control Centre

LSWR   London & South Western Railway

SECR   South Eastern & Chatham Railway

SNCB   Belgian National Railways

SNCF   French National Railways

TMST   Trans Manche Super Train

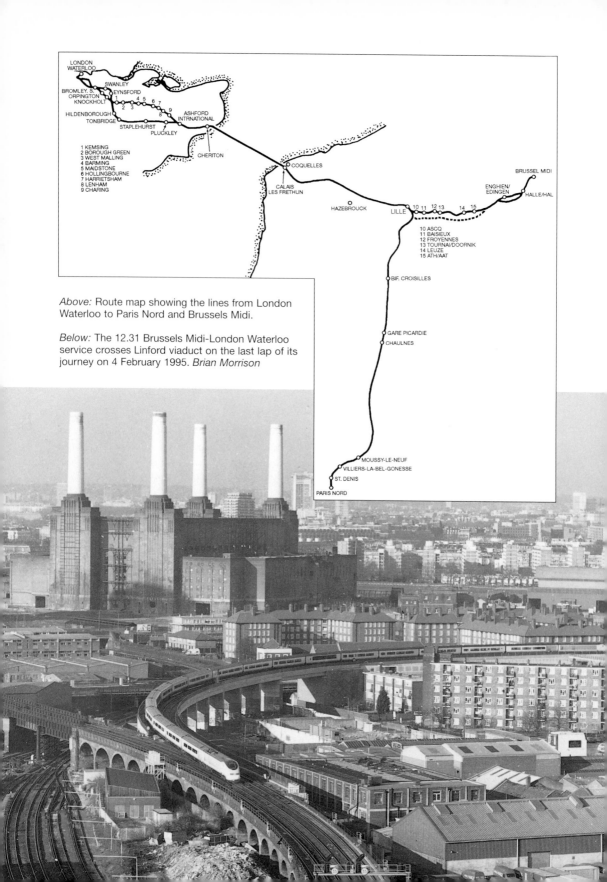

LONDON
WATERLOO
SWANLEY
BROMLEY. S. EYNSFORD
ORPINGTON
KNOCKHOLT 1
4 5 6 7
2 3 9
HILDENBOROUGH 8
TONBRIDGE ASHFORD
STAPLEHURST INTRNATIONAL
PLUCKLEY

1 KEMSING
2 BOROUGH GREEN
3 WEST MALLING
4 BARMING
5 MAIDSTONE
6 HOLLINGBOURNE
7 HARRIETSHAM
8 LENHAM
9 CHARING

CHERITON

COQUELLES

CALAIS
LES FRETHUN

BRUSSEL MIDI

ENGHIEN/
EDINGEN

HALLE/HAL

HAZEBROUCK

LILLE 10 11 12 13 14 15

10 ASCQ
11 BAISIEUX
12 FROYENNES
13 TOURNAI/DOORNIK
14 LEUZE
15 ATH/AAT

BIF. CROISILLES

GARE PICARDIE
CHAULNES

MOUSSY-LE-NEUF
VILLIERS-LA-BEL-GONESSE
ST. DENIS
PARIS NORD

Above: Route map showing the lines from London Waterloo to Paris Nord and Brussels Midi.

Below: The 12.31 Brussels Midi-London Waterloo service crosses Linford viaduct on the last lap of its journey on 4 February 1995. *Brian Morrison*

Introduction

Ever since the end of the last Ice Age, when Britain was separated from continental Europe by the short distance known as the English Channel on this side of the water and La Manche on the other, it has been a dream that, sooner or later, it would be possible, once again, to make a physical connection. For almost two centuries engineers and others have sought to develop proposals that would lead to a successful fixed link; to Napoleon, for example, a Channel crossing would have facilitated a successful invasion by removing at one stroke the supremacy that the Royal Navy enjoyed in defending British waters.

All these proposals, however, came to nothing (although some limited construction was achieved — a proposal of the 1870s saw a tunnel reach some 1.2 miles from Shakespeare Cliff) until the early 1970s, when construction on the first genuine scheme got under way. One factor in the failure of the earlier schemes was the continuing fear of French invasion; although Britain and France had not been to war since 1815, there was still considerable rivalry as each country sought to expand its overseas Empire and even in the late 19th century military commentators could speculate on the likelihood of a French attack across the Channel. It was only with the rise of a united Germany after 1870 and the Anglo-French *Entente Cordiale* of

Right: Typical Eurostar computer originated tickets. This type of ticket will allow passengers to make use of the automated ticket check-in facilities at London Waterloo. Eurostar's ticketing system — 'Tribute' — cost some £17 million and is designed to allow for automatic check-in through the terminals at London, Paris and Brussels as well as the intermediate stations in Ashford, Calais and Lille.

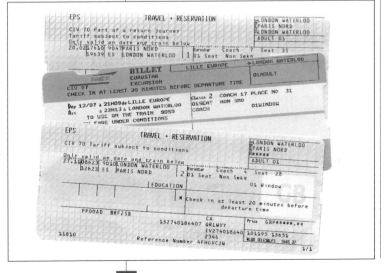

1905 that British military thinking saw Germany replace France as the major threat. Building work on the 1970s scheme proceeded and twin bores were constructed from Shakespeare Cliff at Folkestone for some distance under the sea until, in 1975, the Labour Government of Harold Wilson, suffering from dire financial straits, abruptly terminated the project amidst much controversy. There it seemed the dream would remain — a folly destined never to be completed.

Paradoxically, it was to be the Conservative Government led by Margaret Thatcher — never one renowned for her love of closer connections with Europe — and the Socialist Government of François Mitterrand in France that agreed in 1981 to examine proposals for a fixed link between the two states. A number of options were examined, and in 1986 it was announced that the Anglo-French consortium Eurotunnel had been awarded the franchise. Unlike the aborted 1970s project, in the entrepreneurial 1980s the project was to be funded solely by private capital. Eurotunnel started to raise funds and placed the construction contract with a second consortium Trans Manche Link (TML). With initial funding in place, construction work commenced on both sides of the Channel in 1987. The initial breakthrough occurred on 30 October 1990, when a probe passed through; the historic breakthrough ceremony took place on 1 December the same year. The tunnel was to be opened officially by HM The Queen and French President Mitterrand on 6 May 1994. Following further trials, the Eurotunnel 'Le Shuttle' services were introduced on 22 December 1994 and the through Eurostar services from London to Paris and Brussels were inaugurated on 14 November 1994 — the £9 billion construction project had been brought to a successful conclusion.

Parallel with the construction of the tunnel itself there were other developments essential to the introduction of express trains between London, Paris and Brussels. New station facilities were required. London Waterloo (perhaps only the British could be so perverse as to direct international trains from France into a terminus named after one of the most crushing defeats of French forces in Europe), Paris Gare du Nord and Brussels-Midi were selected as the terminus stations with intermediate facilities at Ashford International, Calais-Fréthun and Lille-Europe. Uniquely, for Britain, the stations at Ashford and Waterloo were to be provided with passport and customs control (although the former is now undertaken on the train).

In France, building of the Channel Tunnel allowed for the construction of the TGV (*Train à Grande Vitesse*) Nord from Paris to Lille and Calais, which was completed and operational for the launch of the Eurostar services in 1994. A high-speed line is under construction from Lille to Brussels; this was

*Above:*The Channel Tunnel was one of the largest construction schemes ever undertaken in Britain. In order to complete the tunnel, vast amounts of precast concrete were dispatched from a plant on the Isle of Grain to reception sidings built at Sevington to the south of Ashford. On 23 March 1988 these trains were launched at a ceremony. 'West Country' Pacific No 34106 *Bodmin* was the star attraction, but air braking for the steam locomotive was provided by this BP Oil 0-6-0 diesel. Approximately 800,000 precast concrete segments were delivered during the construction of the tunnel. *Brian Morrison*

completed in 1997 and travellers using the existing track would have noticed dramatic evidence of the construction as their train heads to or from the Belgian capital. Only in Britain has construction work not started on a high-speed link, although a certain amount of upgrading has taken place on the existing infrastructure between Folkestone and London. The desire of the Conservative Government to provide the high-speed line through the use of private capital, along with controversy over its route through Kent and ultimate terminus in London, has delayed progress, although Union Railways (the British Rail subsidiary tasked with pushing the link through and which is now also part of the London & Continental franchise) is now established and work on the link should be completed in two stages during the first decade of the next century (although developments in early 1998 meant that Railtrack will also have a lead role in the construction of the link). Using the current (1997) infrastructure the fastest times achievable between London and Paris and London and Brussels are three hours and three hours 15min respectively, although this was improved with the completion of the fast line to Belgium at the end of 1997. With this route completed, journey times between London and Brussels will be reduced to two hours 40min, whilst the opening of the British high-speed link will see journey times to

Paris and Brussels reduced to two hours 30min and two hours 10min respectively. In early 1998, however, problems over London & Continental's funding for the high-speed line threw the project back in the melting pot. Following a period of uncertainty, the government announced that a restructured L&CR consortium in conjunction with Railtrack would build the CTRL and the operation of L&CR's part of the Eurostar services would be contracted to a consortium formed of SNCF, SNCB, British Airways and National Express.

There were three partners in the Eurostar consortium: the French National Railways (SNCF), the Belgian National Railways (SNCB) and European Passenger Services (EPS — later Eurostar [UK] Ltd) from Britain. Initially, EPS was established as a wholly-owned subsidiary of the British Railways Board based in offices at Waterloo station. However, the intention of the government was that, alongside the general privatisation of the railways, EPS would pass into the private sector. It was announced in early 1996 that EPS and Union Railways would be sold to a consortium, London & Continental (in which Richard Branson's Virgin Group had a stake), and that this consortium would handle the final development of the Channel Tunnel link and its construction. Other companies involved in the original L&CR group were Ove Arup & Partners, Bechtel Ltd,

Above: One of the North of London Eurostar units — Nos 3308 leading 3307 — is seen at Glasgow's Polmadie depot on 5 June 1997 alongside Virgin Trains' InterCity 125 No 43155. Also pictured is one of Eurostar (UK)'s Class 37/6 locomotives, No 37606. *Colin J. Marsden*

Sir William Halcrow & Partners, National Express Group, SBG Warburg, Systra and London Electricity.

After a period of testing, Eurostar services were launched (not without problems) in November 1994. More than 40 months on, the number of trains operating daily between the three capital cities has grown dramatically (currently there are 14 journeys per weekday from London to Paris, with 16 on Fridays) and traffic has also shown an impressive growth. At the premium end of the market, Eurostar is starting to attract significant numbers of business travellers away from the airlines, and as journey times are further reduced so Eurostar's advantage of centre-to-centre travel will be further improved by journey times that compare favourably with those by air.

When this book started life, there were two further developments that looked as though they were going to extend the influence of passenger traffic through the Channel Tunnel beyond London. The first of these was the acquisition of eight shortened half-sets for use on North of London services. These were planned to serve Glasgow and Edinburgh via the East Coast route and Birmingham, Manchester and Liverpool via the West Coast main line. The North of London sets have been delivered and have been undergoing trials on both the East and West Coast routes, although there is, at the current time, no definite date for their entry into service. Also proposed were sleeper services ('Nightstar'), using locomotive-hauled rakes from Glasgow, Plymouth and Swansea to Paris, Brussels, Amsterdam, Cologne, Frankfurt and Dortmund. A total of 139 coaches have been built; but these are now stored and their entry into service is unlikely in the foreseeable future. Nightstar services were also to involve Dutch and German state railways, in addition to the partners in the existing Eurostar consortium.

The Trains

There are few more technically complicated trains than the Trans Manche Super Trains (TMSTs or Class 373). There is one simple reason for this — they have to cope with three distinct operating voltages and three different methods of railway operation. A whole range of factors had to be taken into consideration in the initial specifications, including the most basic fact that the three countries through which the TMSTs were destined to operate set their passenger platforms at different heights relative to the track.

Just as the operational side was formed of a tripartite international consortium, so the team that was to develop the TMST drew on experience from Britain, France and Belgium. The International Project Group for the international trains was established in 1987 and this set the basic specifications. One consortium, based upon GEC-Alsthom (the Anglo-French engineering company), was contracted to undertake the actual construction of the train units, with the work being spread between contractors in each of the three constituent countries. The actual contract was worth £500 million. The dominance of GEC-Alsthom in the consortium was increased by its acquisition of Metro-Cammell in Birmingham (whose Washwood Heath works was to play an important role in the final assembly of the trains and where a new £5 millions shed was constructed to handle the work) and the Belgian concern ACEC Transport. There were, however, other companies involved; these included Brush in Britain, which built the traction motors, and the French company de Dietrich, which built the body shells for the coaches.

Initially, a contract for 31 units was placed in December 1989. These 31 units were to be divided between France (with 16), Britain (with 11) and Belgium (with four). In addition, European Passenger Services ordered seven shorter sets (14 coaches as opposed to 18 for the 'Three Capitals' sets) for the 'North of London' services. In order to facilitate the development of the TMSTs, a considerable amount of experimental work was undertaken. This work included the fitting of a TMST bogie on a Class 33 diesel-electric (No 33205) in Britain and SNCF No BB10003 was also used as a test-bed.

By early 1991 the construction of the first power cars was under-way at the GEC-Alsthom works at Belfort. The first TMST test set (numbered PS1 — the 'PS'

Above left: The interior of a Standard class coach. Each rake of two sets can accommodate 584 Standard class passengers.

Left: The interior of a First Class coach. First Class accommodation is situated in the centre of the train, comprising coaches Nos 7 to 12, and provides a total of 210 seats. *Brian Morrison*

Left: Each TMST rake of two sets is provided with two bar-buffet coaches (Nos 6 and 13). These act as buffet cars for Standard class passengers and kitchens for the meals served in First class.
Brian Morrison

Below: A rake of Eurostar coaches await completion at GEC-Alsthom's works at Washwood Heath, Birmingham, on 25 May 1994.
Brian Morrison

stood for 'Pre-Series' — and comprising power cars Nos 3001/3002 and seven coaches) emerged from Belfort on 22 January 1993 and its first test run, from Strasbourg Ville, occurred on 28 January 1993. The first recorded run at 100mph took place on the following day. The second test set, No PS2, emerged a few months later. The first TMST crossed through the Channel Tunnel to the UK on 20 June 1993. On 16 October 1993 the first complete UK rake (UK1) was released from Washwood Heath for testing and the first full rake was handed over to EPS on

Above: Eurostar bogies at Washwood Heath on 25 May 1994 during the construction of the TMST sets. *Brian Morrison*

1 November. It was undergoing tests within a week. The first London to Paris TMST run — for staff familiarisation — occurred on 2 June 1994, some five months before the launch of the services. The testing procedure had highlighted a number of problems, of which the circuit breakers being tripped during third-rail operation due to a rogue 50Hz frequency was but one.

Technology

In terms of electric supply, each TMST set is required to be able to operate at three different voltages: there is the 750V dc third-rail of the existing line from Waterloo to the Channel Tunnel there is the 3kV dc overhead of SNCB; and there is the 25kV ac used both in the tunnel itself and on SNCF. An additional complication is that there are three different standards of 25kV overhead, and the pantographs must be able to accommodate these variations. For a train travelling from Britain to France the first of the 25kV sections to be encountered is that adopted by Eurotunnel; the overhead here is set at a much higher level above the track than that elsewhere to allow for the clearance of the Eurotunnel truck shuttles. The second 25kV standard encountered is that of the LGV, where the overhead is set at a fixed height of 5.10m — albeit with very slight variations — and the pantograph head is set at a fixed height which restricts its movement. Finally, there is the standard 25kV, where the level of the overhead can fluctuate above the track and for which a fully mobile pantograph is required. In traffic the changes between voltage and pick-up equipment have to be undertaken with the train in motion, and each TMST cab is equipped with two switches, operated by the driver, that enable the changeover to be achieved without disturbing the passengers or delaying the train.

The three voltages do not generate the same power output. This is best shown in the table below. In each case the weight of the train is 752 tonnes.

This power equates, at 25kV, to 20.4hp/tonne; this is considerably less than the TGV-Nord sets (30.8hp/tonne) which means that the TMST sets face potentially greater speed variations over the gradients on the LGV-Nord and, therefore, require greater skill on the part of the drivers to ensure a smooth ride for the passengers. The maximum power of 16,408hp, generated by the 12 asynchronous motors, is available only when operating at 25kV. Each power car is provided with two

Power Supply	Power Generated (MW)	kW/Tonne
25kV	12.2	16.2
3kV	5.7	7.6
750V	3.4	4.5

Below: Completed TMST sets await delivery outside Washwood Heath on 25 May 1994. The power car illustrated, No 3108, heads the last of eight rakes to be based in Brussels.
Brian Morrison

pantographs, one for operation on the 25kV lines and one for the Belgian 3kV system. Six axles — the four on the power car and the outer two on the leading coaches (R1 and R18) are powered and each has two bogies with two retractable shoes for use on the 750V dc lines in Britain. Each bogie has a wheelbase of 3,000mm and the bogie centres are 14m apart on the power car and 18.7m between that on the leading coach and the power car.

Another problem faced by the designers of the train was that Britain and Europe lacked a common standard in terms of platform height. In France and Belgium the platforms are set at 550mm (21.6in) and 760mm (30in) respectively above track level, whilst in Britain platforms are much higher (at 915mm/36in). This problem was resolved by the incorporation of retractable steps which can be lowered in France and Belgium but which are not required in Britain.

The trains are fitted with two distinct methods of braking. The first is friction. Each of the non-powered wheelsets is fitted with disc brakes, whilst each of the powered axles is fitted with brake shoes; the latter also help to keep the tyres clean. The friction braking is pneumatically

Below: The interior of the cab of a TMST showing the central worktop position with the push-pull power and brake controllers located on either side. Ahead of the worktop and beneath the window is the TVM430 display; beneath the TVM430 display and largely obscured by the worktop is the ribbon-type speedometer. The two foot pedals are two of the six vigilance positions with which the TMST cab is fitted; the driver rests his feet on these pedals and when he receives the periodic signal has to respond within a given time or the circuit breakers are applied. To the right of the control console – but not yet fitted here – is the cab-shore radio equipment. Directly above this are the two rotational switches used by the driver to vary the voltage and power supply equipment. To the left of the worktop are various gauges which provide the driver with information such as air pressure. *GEC-Alsthom*

operated and is used only on speeds of less than 25mph (40km/h) or in an emergency. For braking at higher speeds, each train is also fitted with rheostatic braking. This effectively turns the traction motors into generators, with the power thus generated dissipated as heat through rheostatic braking stacks located at the outer ends of the leading coaches (R1 and R18). The computer system ensures that both systems of braking are effectively co-ordinated to ensure smooth braking. At the maximum speed of 186mph (300km/h), the train will stop in 2.2 miles (3.5km).

From the primary power supply, the electricity supply to the coaches is stepped down through four Train Auxiliary Choppers (TACs) — which are located in coaches R5/R8/R11/R14 — to 530V dc to power auxiliary equipment such as battery chargers, train heating and air compressors. This power supply is further modified through 250kVA inverters to provide a supply at 380V ac for other electrical equipment and air conditioning.

The trailing coaches are all constructed in monocoque form — ie without a chassis — and were built to smaller than UIC standard loading gauge to accommodate the fact that Britain's gauge is smaller than that in Europe. This means that the roof height is reduced by some 33cm and the width by 8.6cm. The streamlined nose section is constructed from glass reinforced plastic,

Right: A close-up of two of the coach ends shows the articulation of the bogies at this point. *Author*

Below: Two R1 vehicles, Nos 733041 and 733031, for Eurostar sets stand in a train consist at Dollands Moor on 13 October 1995 for delivery to GEC-Alsthom at Washford Heath. *Brian Morrison*

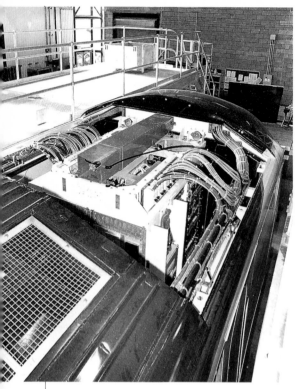

moulded to shape. Behind this, the driver is provided with a steel safety cage with a crumple zone for protection in the case of any accident.

The driver's position is located centrally behind the single-piece windscreen. Although the technology looks daunting, the primary part of the control system is the box located directly in front of him. This has handles on either side which move forward for acceleration and back for braking. In another nice touch, the speedometer displays mph when travelling in Britain and km/h when running in Europe.

Left: As part of the programme of testing the TMST sets, the Pre-Series rake was used on the Strasbourg-Selestat line of SNCF. It is seen here departing from Strasbourg on 28 January 1993. *David Haydock*

Above: The same rake is seen at Selestat on 28 January 1993 at the conclusion of its successful run from Strasbourg. *David Haydock*

Right: During one of the many pre-commissioning runs, TMST No 3205 stands at Arras *en route* for Paris Gare du Nord on 13 April 1994. This was the first occasion that passengers had travelled in a Eurostar train. *Colin J. Marsden*

Above: The first completed Eurostar rake arrived in England at 08.30 on 20 June 1994 after being hauled through the Channel Tunnel by SNCF electric locomotive No 68041. This is the view at the English portal when the set arrived and had to receive clearance from HM Customs before continuing its journey to North Pole depot.
Colin J. Marsden

Below: Prior to the introduction of Eurostar services, there was considerable training of the crews. To facilitate route learning, a two-car unit, converted from a withdrawn Class 2-EPB unit, was utilised. No 931001 is pictured approaching Otford Junction with a trip from Folkestone to Clapham Junction on 13 January 1994.
Chris Wilson

The Route

lthough the French authorities ensured that the flagship Eurostar services would operate over a high-speed line from their inauguration, in both Belgium and Britain delays meant that in neither country were the new services to operate on new lines. In Belgium the high-speed lines were being constructed with a view to completion during 1997, but in Britain the new fast link to the Channel Tunnel is now not destined to be completed until the early years of the 21st century.

The British terminus for Eurostar was designated as Waterloo, where a new International station with five platforms was constructed in place of the platforms that served the Windsor lines. Before the International station, with its specific requirements (customs hall, etc), could be completed, the existing main line station had to undergo considerable modification. This work, which included the demolition of the familiar signalbox, the removal of the original Windsor lines platforms, the building of two additional platforms in the domestic station (in place of the taxi road) and the loss of the lift for Waterloo & City stock, was undertaken between 1988 and 1990. The new station, designed by Nicholas Grimshaw, was constructed between December 1990 and its official opening on 6 May 1993, along with new lines from International Junction. The

original scheduled date for the opening of the Channel Tunnel was 15 May 1993 but, in reality, services did not commence from the £130 million terminus for another 18 months. Although Waterloo main line station is owned by Railtrack, the International station itself is owned by Eurostar (UK) Ltd, and is one of the assets transferred to the London & Continental consortium.

From International Junction to Nine Elms Junction, Eurostar services intersperse with South West Trains services running over the ex-LSWR main line through Vauxhall. This line, now much widened, first operated on 11 July 1848 when the LSWR opened its extension from its terminus at Nine Elms to the new Waterloo station. At Nine Elms Junction, the trains ascend over the new Stewarts Lane Viaduct; this viaduct, opened in 1994, was one of the only significant infrastructure additions to the route between London and Folkestone. At Linford Street Junction Eurostar services join the 'Chatham' lines from Victoria. From this point, as far as the Eurotunnel complex at Cheriton, the train operates over the metals of the former SECR (including both ex-South Eastern and ex-London, Chatham & Dover lines). The section of line opened from Stewarts Lane Junction to Herne Hill on 25 August 1862, thence to Beckenham (Penge Junction) on 1 July 1863. The line from Penge Junction to Shortlands, via

Beckenham Junction, had opened earlier, on 3 May 1858. At Shortlands the Eurostar services take the line through Bromley South to Bickley which opened on 5 July 1858. The Bickley Junction-Petts Wood Junction line, which allows Eurostar services access to the main line through Orpington to Tonbridge, was opened in September 1902; this was another site where there was much engineering work to accommodate the new services. The line through Orpington to Sevenoaks opened for public services on 3 March 1868. It was extended to Tonbridge on 1 June 1868. The line from Tonbridge — at the time called Maidstone Road — to Paddock Wood opened on 31 August 1842 and thence to Ashford on the following 1 December. The final section of the erstwhile SECR covered by the Eurostar services is that from Ashford to Continental Junction, Folkestone, which was opened by the South Eastern Railway on 28 June 1843.

As can be seen, with the exception of the Stewarts Lane Viaduct, Eurostar services in England operate over lines that are, for the most part, more than 125 years old. Although there was some upgrading prior to the launch of the flagship services (55 bridges, for example, required modification along the route), Eurostar services are constrained both by the speed limits of the conventional lines in and by the frequency of passenger services

Below: Waterloo International: the 400m-long train shed of the International platforms snakes out westwards beyond the domestic platforms towards International Junction. *Eurostar (UK) Ltd*

Above: Passing newly-erected sound reflecting fencing at Bromley South on 14 January 1996, the 14.10 Waterloo-Gare du Nord Eurostar is formed of one of the French-owned rakes, Nos 3213 and 3214. *Brian Morrison*

operated by the three main Train Operating Companies in the region — South West Trains, Connex South Central and Connex South Eastern — as well as the increasing freight traffic to and from the Channel Tunnel with which Eurostar shares its tracks.

Once through the Channel Tunnel, however, it is a completely different story so far as France is concerned. The high-speed line linking Calais with Lille and Paris — the LGV-Nord Europe — was constructed to facilitate not only Eurostar services, but also French domestic TGV services to Lille and the new international Thalys services linking Paris with Brussels and Amsterdam. The LGV-Nord Europe was opened on 23 May 1993 (initially from Paris to Arras, thence to Lille over conventional lines until the completion of the section from Arras to Lille) and, to the

east of Lille, provides a direct link into the Belgian high-speed line, which was under construction at the time of this book's compilation and to which further reference will be found in the chapter dealing with the trip between Lille and Brussels.

As in Britain, until the completion of the new high-speed line, Eurostar services in Belgium are forced to utilise the existing SNCF/SNCB route between Lille and Brussels-Midi. The line from Lille to Froyennes was opened on 1 December 1865. The French-Belgian border is situated just to the east of Baisieux, although travellers would be hard-pressed to spot any great difference except that peering out of the window to adjacent roads, there are now more cars labelled 'B' than 'F'! At Froyennes, Eurostar services join the Mouscron-Tournai line; this route opened on 24 October 1842. The existing station at Tournai was opened on 15 February 1870, with the opening of the line from Tournai to Mons via Basécles. Eurostar services, however, head almost due east from Tournai over the line to Maffle via Leuze, which was opened on 30 October

Left: The 12.27 Waterloo International-Brussels service glides through Orpington on 11 February 1995. The train is formed of Nos 3013 (leading) and 3012. The presence of a domestic EMU in the platform is a vivid reminder that, until the completion of the Channel Tunnel Rail Link, Eurostar services have to be diagrammed amongst the existing passenger services to Kent. Despite the improvements undertaken to increase line speed and capacity, it is not unknown for services to be held at signals. *Brian Morrison*

Centre left: Passing beneath the new Ashford bypass at Sevington, the 08.10 Waterloo-Paris service heads south on 6 October 1996. Le Landy-allocated No 3229 heads No 3230. *Brian Morrison*

Below left: The 12.12 Paris-Waterloo Eurostar joins the Railtrack main line from Ashford to Dover at Continental Junction on 17 March 1995. The train is formed of Nos 3205 (leading) and 3204. In the background can be seen the impressive freight yard at Dollands Moor, with two SNCF Class 22xxx locomotives, Nos 22380 and 22404, and two Class 92s, Nos 92023 *Ravel* and 92023 *Charles Dickens*, awaiting their next duties. *Brian Morrison*

Below: Destination of the Eurostar services to Paris is Gare du Nord; here, on 13 April 1994 No 3206 prepares to head to Arras on a training run. *Colin J. Marsden*

1847. From Maffle, Eurostar services take the line through Silly *(sic)* and Edingen to Halle. At Halle, the original line from Brussels to Maffle via Jurbise is met.

Until the completion of the high-speed line through Belgium, Eurostar services are, again like those in Britain, subject to the constraints of lower speed limits than on the LGV and the proximity of standard SNCB traffic.

Although the French terminus at Gare du Nord was to be accommodated within the existing train shed, considerable preparatory work was required for the high-speed era, since Gare du Nord would also act as the terminus for both the TGV-Nord services and the later Thalys operations to Belgium and the Netherlands. Much investment went into the rebuilding of the old Le Landy depot to both house and maintain the French-allocated units, but there was also a great deal of work required in track realignment and platform construction.

The rear of a Brussels-bound Eurostar heads northwards at Forest-Midi in mid-1997 over SNCB's old route 96A. The construction of the Belgian high-speed line has, since its opening in late 1997, radically reduced the journey times between London and Brussels. *Alan F. Reekie*

Servicing the Train

The unit that will form our train is one of the UK-based sets allocated to North Pole International depot; this is one of three depots that handle the 'Three Capitals' stock. The other two are Le Landy (Paris) and Forest (Brussels) which are owned by SNCF and SNCB respectively. North Pole International is situated alongside the Great Western main line from Paddington and is accessed by a link off the Clapham Junction-Kensington Olympia-Willesden Junction (West London) route. Of the 31 TMST sets 11 are allocated to North Pole, 16 to Le Landy and four to Forest.

To the west of the West London line are situated the reception sidings. Access to these is via electronically-controlled gates at which trains pass from the control of

Victoria powerbox to North Pole control; at this point the units also transfer from the third-rail of the West London line to the 25kV overhead used within the depot area, and from the control of the IECC at Victoria to North Pole's own Control Centre. During its stay at North Pole, each set has an individual reporting number. There are four reception sidings; one of these is equipped with a 3,000V dc power supply for testing of equipment used when running in Belgium. These give access either to the stabling sidings or to the carriage washing plant; the carriage washing plant is equipped with a chemical wash and a rinse. In order to access the carriage washer, the front pantograph is lowered and the train receives power from the rear pantograph only; once the front power car

Left: The scale of the North Pole International complex can be gauged from this view of an InterCity 125 proceeding from Old Oak Common to Paddington to form the 17.10 service to Hereford on 29 December 1994. Visible on the extreme right, beyond the stabled TMST sets, can be seen the 400m-long servicing shed. *Brian Morrison*

Right: The exterior of the four-road maintenance building at North Pole International depot. *Brian Morrison*

has passed through the washer, its pantograph is raised and that at the rear of the train is lowered. Beyond the carriage washing unit is the toilet discharge siding; TMST sets are fitted with retention toilets that are usually flushed and disinfected once every three days maximum. The toilet discharge normally takes about 45min. Also on the west side of the depot is the six-road servicing shed.

The servicing shed, which is 400m long, handles the routine servicing of the units and the daily checks required for the maintenance schedule. The servicing shed is

Above left: North Pole International depot is capable of handling all aspects of TMST maintenance. This building houses the wheel lathe. *Brian Morrison*

Left: This is the interior of the maintenance building at North Pole International showing some of the 27 lifting jacks. This equipment allows for one complete set to be raised simultaneously. *Brian Morrison*

Below: Eurostar sets Nos 3005 and 3006 undergo maintenance at North Pole International depot on 14 February 1995. *Brian Morrison*

Above: With its nose covers slid open, No 3102 gives a front end view of the Scharfenburg coupling. Alongside is No 3018 on 14 February 1995. *Brian Morrison*

Below: The unique Scharfenburg coupling-fitted Class 73, No 73130, is seen at North Pole International on 14 February 1995 in the company of TMST units Nos 3019 and 3106. *Brian Morrison*

provided with six roads, of which Nos 5 and 6 are fitted with an overhead crane. All tests are undertaken in the 25kV mode. From the west side of the site there are two links: one line provides access into the southbound West London line for trains entering service; the second line provides a link with the east side of the North Pole complex, where there are situated the repair shed, the bogie drop and the wheel lathe. Each of the four roads of the repair shed can accommodate a full set; it takes roughly 30min for the TMST set to be divided into the two half-sets. One road of the repair shed is equipped with 26

synchronised jacks, most with a capacity of 20 tonnes, that enable all 10 vehicles of a TMST set to be jacked up simultaneously. Also situated at North Pole is the International Supply Centre. This facility cost £3 million and was opened by the then Managing Director of EPS, Richard Edgeley, on 14 February 1995. The Supply Centre is designed to hold some 12,000 parts, ranging from transformers used in power cars to consumables (such as soap) used in service. The computer stock control is compatible with that used by both Le Landy and Forest and, if necessary, smaller items can be carried from one depot to another on board a TMST. In order to facilitate the operation of North Pole depot, there are two ex-British Rail locomotives — Nos 08948 and 73130 — which are fitted with Scharfenburg couplings.

The maintenance schedule is as follows:

Below: Access to Waterloo International from North Pole International is via the West London line. On 9 September 1995 TMST sets Nos 3002 and 3001 pass through Kensington Olympia station working ECS back to North Pole depot. *Chris Wilson*

Maintenance schedule

ESA	*Examen de Sortie d'Atelier*	Ex-Works examination.
VIC	*Visite d'Initialisation du Cycle*	Brief examination at start of cycle.
ES	*Examen en Service*	Daily (maximum 2,500km, or 1,600km for sustained high-speed running). The *ES* is undertaken overnight and requires approximately 12-20 man hours. It is little more than a visual examination of the train's exterior and underneath.
ECF	*Examen Confort*	Seven days (maximum nine days). This is an examination of the train's interior.
VOR	*Visite des Organes de Roulement*	Seven days (maximum nine days). This includes an examination of the brakes and the third-rail power shoes.
ATS	*Autres Travaux Systématiques*	Monthly (coinciding with every fourth *VOR*). This is primarily an examination of the wheel sets. Currently it involves the jacking up of each individual axle and the rotation of the wheel sets to ensure that they are correctly formed.
VL	*Visite Limitée*	Three months (plus two weeks maximum). This is undertaken in the Maintenance Workshop and requires all the checks undertaken in the more frequent examinations combined with tests for the brakes and doors. A set undergoing a *VL* will be taken out of service for a full day, and 180 man-hours of labour is allocated to the job.
VG	*Visite Générale*	Six months (plus two weeks maximum). This requires the train to be out of service for three working days and has 500 man-hours allocated to it. One of the roads in the Maintenance Workshop is fitted with a 25kV power supply to facilitate testing of equipment.
SIV	*Spécial Intérieur Voiture*	Nine months.
GVG	*Grande Visite Générale*	18 months (plus two weeks maximum). This will require the train to be out of service for five working days. Given that the operation is now more than three years old, most units have probably undergone two *GVG* examinations.
OPCE	*Operation de Confort Esthétique*	Eight years. This is designed for a major examination of each train's interior.
MI-VIE	Mid-life refurbishment	Approximately 15 years.

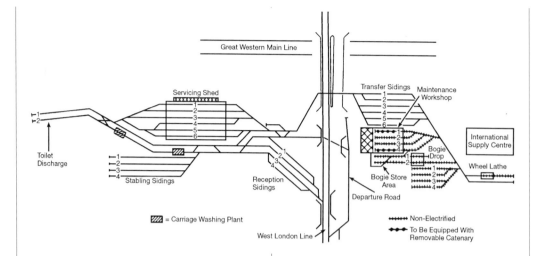

Great Western Main Line

Servicing Shed

Transfer Sidings

Maintenance Workshop

International Supply Centre

Bogie Drop

Wheel Lathe

Toilet Discharge

Stabling Sidings

Reception Sidings

Bogie Store Area

Departure Road

////// = Carriage Washing Plant

West London Line

++++++ Non-Electrified

●●●●● To Be Equipped With Removable Catenary

Above: Track diagram of North Pole depot.

Below: North Pole handles the maintenance of Eurostar trains in the UK; in France maintenance is handled by Le Landy and in Belgium by Forest. Here Eurostar set No 3205 stands inside Le Landy shed reception area on 11 June 1996. The depot also handles the maintenance of the TGV-R and Thalys sets. *Colin J. Marsden*

The maintenance schedule is the same for all TMST units, irrespective of ownership and is co-ordinated by the Comité International de Maintenance Eurostar. The *ECF* and *VOR* examinations are normally undertaken simultaneously. The schedule is designed for the full life of the train, although as the units are only four years old, it will be some time before Eurostar needs to implement either of the last two stages. The schedule of maintenance from *ES* through to *ATS* is planned for completion in the servicing shed; the heavier work is undertaken or will be undertaken in the repair shed. North Pole has the capacity to handle 18 sets per night.

The unit to form our train arrived from Paris the previous evening. After having disgorged its passengers at Waterloo International, it made its way back through Vauxhall, past Nine Elms Junction and Queenstown Road station, before taking the West London Junction-Latchmere No 3 Junction — the newly-reinstated Sheepcote Lane chord — to gain access to the West London line. Travelling via Kensington Olympia, the train entered the North Pole International yard.

Having entered the reception sidings the train was routed via the carriage washers to the toilet discharge point. Having been fully cleansed, it was then taken through the servicing shed for its overnight examination. Although the basic parameters for the maintenance schedule are outlined above, as a train operates so the crew can identify particular faults that require rectification; these repairs are also undertaken at this time. With the train fully serviced and with any faults rectified, it is now ready for operation.

Although this section has concentrated on the North Pole facility — as this is where our train for today was initially prepared — Eurostar sets are also maintained at depots in France and Belgium. The French facility, owned by SNCF, is situated at Le Landy, just to the north of Gare du Nord. Le Landy handles the maintenance, not only of the Eurostar sets, but also the TGVs that operate over the LGV-Nord and the international Thalys sets for use on the routes to Amsterdam and Cologne. Le Landy is the biggest of the three sites and covers an area of some 30 hectares. In order to handle the Eurostar sets, Le Landy is provided with a three-track 400m-long

shed. The Belgian facility, Forest, is owned by SNCB and is located on the southern approaches to Midi station. This depot was based on an earlier EMU depot that had closed in October 1990 for conversion. As with Le Landy, Forest is also tasked with the maintenance of the Thalys sets. Of the Eurostar rakes, 22 sets (ie 11 complete trains) are allocated to North Pole — Nos 3001-3022 — 32 sets (16 complete trains) to Le Landy — Nos 3201-32 — and eight (four complete trains) to Brussels — Nos 3101-08. The eight shortened sets (four complete trains) of North of London stock, Nos 3301-08, were to be allocated to North Pole.

Below: In the build-up to the introduction of North of London services, a series of link trains from Waterloo to those destinations to be served by the NoL services, such as Edinburgh and Manchester, was operated; these services have been subsequently withdrawn. One of these connecting services, formed of an InterCity 125 set, crosses the River Thames at Chelsea Wharf. Eurostar rakes to and from North Pole also traverse this bridge on their approach to Clapham Junction.
Eurostar (UK) Ltd

Preparations for Departure

Our train, No 9010, is formed of TMST sets Nos 3021 and 3022 which are based at North Pole International. Although the passengers are told to check in at least 20min prior to departure, our train has been sitting at platform 23 for more than an hour alongside a second rake of TMST sets that will form train No 9116 to Brussels. This second train is due to depart from Waterloo at 08.27, some four minutes after our scheduled departure. The period before departure allows for the driver to run through the programmed checks to ensure that all systems are operational. With a train as complicated as the TMST — it has to satisfy the operational requirements of three very distinct railway operators — the checks can take a significant amount of time.

Our driver, being English, logs into the system and selects the English language option. There are, inevitably, French and Flemish options as well. Initially the check

Above left: A view from the buffer stops at Waterloo International sees TMST set No 3008 under the dramatic lines of the station's overall roof on 22 July 1994. *Brian Morrison*

Left: Pictured along the platform towards the buffer stops, TMST sets Nos 3004 and 3003 are pictured at Waterloo International on 14 February 1994 during the test programme prior to the introduction of services. *Brian Morrison*

involves fault diagnosis and any modifications that have been undertaken, either temporary or permanent. This process, which involves scanning a series of pages on a computer screen is currently undertaken manually, but it is expected that eventually it will be completed automatically. There are a series of different levels of page: the 'M' pages record standard information whilst the 'R' pages record those things that have occurred during the preceding journey and provide information for the fitters to facilitate repairs. Given that our unit has spent the night being checked at North Pole following its arrival on a service from Brussels the previous day, it comes as little surprise that there is nothing of significance noted. In addition to the computer, there is also a manual check book, which is examined for any supplementary information.

As the train will be travelling too fast through France on the high-speed line to use conventional signalling, the TMST sets are equipped with the French TVM430 system (as also used on the TGVs). 'TVM' is an abbreviation of *Transmission Voie Machine* (which is translated as Track to Train Transmission). This equipment, which is situated at the front of the cab ahead of the main controller, consists of two rows of displays which are activated by normal track circuits. These circuits can

identify the presence of the train and the distance that the train will take to stop. It will then indicate the maximum speed that the train can be driven at to ensure safe operation. In the event that the train is gaining on a slower moving or stationary train ahead, the TVM430 will show an ever-decreasing maximum speed to which the driver must respond. The machine indicates the new lower speed limit one block section before it must be implemented. If the driver fails to respond by the start of the appropriate block section, the TVM430 will automatically apply the brakes.

On the TVM430 there are three distinct colours utilised. Displays with a green background indicate the maximum speed permitted over the line. Those with a

Above: The dramatic lines of the curved roof at Waterloo International are shown to good effect in this view of Eurostar Nos 3106 (closest to the buffer stops) and 3105 at the country end on 25 October 1994. *Brian Morrison*

black background show the maximum permitted speed for the train, whilst those with a white background are to provide the driver with a warning. As there are no anomalies with the TVM430 on this train, our driver is able to validate the equipment.

Following the testing of the TVM430 the driver next tests the VACMA, which is the French vigilance and deadman system. There are six deadman positions in the cab of each TMST. There are two pedals, two touch-sensitive pads (one on each side of the main control box) and two buttons (one on each side of the cab). If the driver fails to retain contact with any of these six points during the train's journey, then the brakes will be automatically applied after six seconds. The vigilance system will issue an aural warning within 50sec to which the driver must respond within three seconds or again the brakes will be automatically applied.

The next piece of equipment to be tested is the TBL or Belgian ATP system. Although our train will not be entering SNCB's network it is still necessary to ensure that this system is working. The TBL issues a warning sign prior to the opening of the circuit breakers and a brake application after 35sec. In reality, the TBL would alert the signal control who would check with the driver. Again the system is found to be correct and our driver is able to reset the circuit breakers for the next test.

The French system of ATP, known as KVB, is next to be tested. This again causes the circuit breakers to trip and the brakes to be applied automatically. Again the test confirms that the system is fully operational.

In an emergency, the driver would switch the headlights of the train so that they flashed instead of issuing a constant beam. In theory, this should also be tested, but the regulations state that this emergency signal should not be tested in an area where other trains are running and, given the frequency of incoming and outgoing trains at Waterloo, it is not practical to undertake this particular test.

The next part of the equipment to be tested is the radio. All TMST sets are equipped with cab to shore radio equipment. Again there are differing types to ensure compatibility with operational requirements in Britain, France and Belgium. A computer print-out confirms that all the systems are functioning correctly. Our driver is now able to enter the signal number into the computer. This is logged by Wimbledon box against the train number and the train number is then utilised throughout the whole journey.

The driver now tests the emergency brake application. After six seconds the brakes are applied and a warning light is illuminated. With the test successfully completed the equipment is isolated. Next to be tested are the French and Belgian equivalent of AWS and ATC; this gives the driver a yellow flashing light.

In theory, at this stage the driver should undertake a brake continuity test, but he is unable to raise immediately a colleague over the internal telephone link to undertake the test in the cab of the rear unit. If no one can be found, the driver will have to walk the full length of the train to complete the test. Whilst waiting for his colleague to return, our driver makes use of the cab radio to contact the signalman at Wimbledon: 'This is the driver of Eurostar train standing at platform 23 at Waterloo International. Just ringing for a radio reception test.' The signalman at Wimbledon responds that reception is loud and clear.

We are now approaching the end of the test procedure. The colleague has returned and the brake continuity test is successfully concluded, our driver requesting his partner to 'hit the plunger'. With this final check completed, our driver can confirm to the train captain that all is ready: 'Tests are complete. Ready for loading.'

It is now some 15min before departure. In the departure lounge expectant passengers have bought their newspapers and guidebooks and are looking at their watches and waiting for the announcement about boarding. The catering crews have got the prepared breakfasts and trolleys on board. Everything is ready for the escalators to be opened and for the passengers to make their ascent to the platform.

Above: Almost a full house at Waterloo International shortly after midday on 11 June 1997. In the background, Class 421/5 '4CIG' No 1304 departs from the domestic station with the 12.20 service for Portsmouth Harbour. *Brian Morrison*

Below: With the departures board announcing that check-in for the 08.23 service to Paris is open, passengers make their way through to the departure lounge at Waterloo International. *Author*

Departure

It is quarter past eight and the last passengers are making their way along the platform and to their seats. Over the PA the Train Captain announces: 'This Eurostar service is about to depart and the doors will close automatically in a few moments.' The message is repeated in French; one of the nice touches on the train is that all announcements are made first in the language of the country through which the train is running. There are further announcements regarding the careful storage of luggage and a welcome to passengers. In the cab our driver is ready for the off.

So far as passengers are concerned, the first indication that the train is about to depart comes with the slight clunk as the automatic doors are closed. Unless there is an emergency, the next time that these doors will be opened will be some three and a half hours later when the train arrives in Paris Gare du Nord. Until the passengers have finally disembarked in Paris they will remain effectively under British jurisdiction; in the reverse direction the French have control from Gare du Nord to Waterloo.

The time is now almost 08.23 — our scheduled time of departure — and Wimbledon box has given our driver the green light to proceed. In addition to the green signal, there is also the illuminated sign 'WR' which indicates that we are being routed via the Windsor Reversible route, the northernmost of the three lines that TMST sets are cleared to use on the approaches to Waterloo station. Immediately adjacent to the green signal is a large speed restriction sign emphasising that our train is limited to 20mph as it negotiates the station throat.

With the doors shut and the green signal, our driver gently eases the power controller forward. Our 394m-long train starts to snake its way out of Waterloo International towards International Junction. Once clear of the platform end we can accelerate slightly to 25mph. In theory, once passed the junction the train can accelerate to the line speed of 60mph, but although our driver does increase the speed fractionally as we depart amidst the heavy commuter traffic that shares the lines into Waterloo at this time in the morning, the speed restriction through the curves at Vauxhall (35mph) means that there is little purpose in accelerating too heavily. Our train passes through Vauxhall station platform 1 (at 08.27); on the adjacent platforms a Class 455 is standing at platform 8 with an outbound service.

About half a mile after Vauxhall station we arrive at Nine Elms Junction. We cross over from the Windsor Reversible line to the approach to the Nine Elms flyover at 45mph. When the flyover was constructed the original up Windsor line was slewed to the north to allow for the construction of

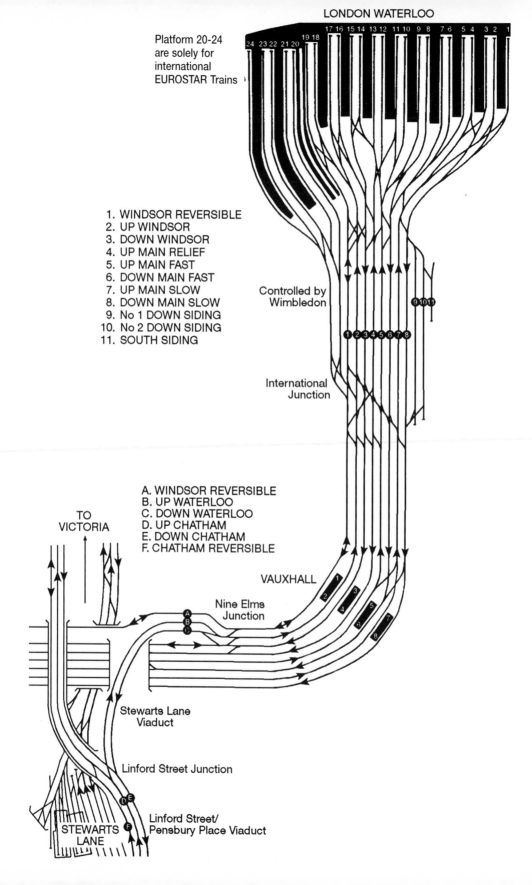

LONDON WATERLOO

24 23 22 21 20 19 18 17 16 15 14 13 12 11 10 9 8 7 6 5 4 3 2 1

Platform 20-24
are solely for
international
EUROSTAR Trains

1. WINDSOR REVERSIBLE
2. UP WINDSOR
3. DOWN WINDSOR
4. UP MAIN RELIEF
5. UP MAIN FAST
6. DOWN MAIN FAST
7. UP MAIN SLOW
8. DOWN MAIN SLOW
9. No 1 DOWN SIDING
10. No 2 DOWN SIDING
11. SOUTH SIDING

Controlled by
Wimbledon

International
Junction

A. WINDSOR REVERSIBLE
B. UP WATERLOO
C. DOWN WATERLOO
D. UP CHATHAM
E. DOWN CHATHAM
F. CHATHAM REVERSIBLE

TO
VICTORIA

VAUXHALL

Nine Elms
Junction

Stewarts Lane
Viaduct

Linford Street Junction

STEWARTS
LANE

Linford Street/
Pensbury Place Viaduct

Left: The platform arrangement at London Waterloo; the domestic trains utilise platforms Nos 1-19 whilst the Eurostar services use the segregated platforms Nos 20-24. From International Junction, the Eurostar trains share tracks with services into and out of the domestic station through Vauxhall to Nine Elms Junction. From Nine Elms Junction Eurostar services cross over the ex-LSWR lines and join the ex-SECR route from Victoria at Linford Street Junction.

Above: Eurostar trains enter and depart from Waterloo International over a new viaduct constructed immediately to the west of Waterloo station. Control of this section of track is undertaken by Wimbledon box for the short distance until trains gain access to the Nine Elms flyover. On 14 February 1994 TMST sets Nos 3003 and 3004 gain access to the new platforms. *Brian Morrison*

the two-track viaduct. We start the ascent of the flyover at 08.29; the building of the flyover, which provides a direct link between the Waterloo-Clapham Junction and Victoria-Wandsworth Road lines, was one of the major construction schemes necessary once Waterloo had been designated as the London terminus for Eurostar services. The sharpness of the curve as we pass over the running lines into Waterloo and the length of the train can give passengers a spectacular view.

It is whilst we cross the Nine Elms flyover that we move from Wimbledon's control to that exercised by Victoria. The first indication of the new regime comes with the signal we meet controlling access at Linford Street Junction. Here the ex-South Eastern & Chatham Railway lines from Victoria are joined. To our right, the large shed at Stewarts Lane is visible. Alongside the numerous locomotives that seem to be stored are two celebrity engines — the green-liveried Class 33 No 33008 *Eastleigh* (which has since been withdrawn and sold for preservation) and the Pullman-liveried Class 73 No 73101 *Brighton Evening Argus*. Factory Junction is passed at 08.30.30. Our train is routed over the down Chatham Fast, which means that it misses the platform roads at Wandsworth

Road and Clapham High Street. At Brixton Junction the line to Denmark Hill heads east, whilst our train heads southeast through Brixton (08.33) and under Atlantic Road viaduct; the line towards Denmark Hill and thence over the Catford Loop is used as an alternative route for Eurostar services (see Chapter 10).

Immediately after Brixton, our driver, who has been faced with adverse signals since Factory Junction is forced to apply the brakes. One of the problems with running the Eurostar services over the congested metals of southeast London is that there is always the possibility of being held up on the approach to one of the many junctions and, indeed, we draw to a stop at the signal governing Herne Hill North Junction at 08.34. We are held for some 15sec whilst an inbound service heading towards London on the up Holborn line clears the junction. Although this section is cleared for 60mph running by

TMSTs, we have barely got above 30mph since leaving Brixton. Whilst we stand at the signal, a 12-car EMU, with No 1841 bringing up the rear, passes as it takes the up Chatham Main towards Victoria.

With the signal cleared, we are able to proceed again and our driver slowly accelerates. We pass through platform 3 at Herne Hill station shortly after 08.36. At Herne Hill South Junction, the up and down Holborn lines head off towards Tulse Hill, whilst we maintain our southeasterly direction passing under the Tulse Hill-Peckham Rye line. Through the junction, we are able to accelerate towards the

60mph speed limit. We pass an inbound EMU formed of a Class 465 unit before passing West Dulwich station at 08.38. To our left we can see the impressive buildings of Dulwich College stretching out amidst its playing fields. Immediately before entering Penge Tunnel (at 08.39) we pass through Sydenham Hill station. Penge Tunnel, at one mile 381yd in length, is the longest tunnel between London and the Channel Tunnel. It is also situated at the summit of the three-mile climb from Brixton.

Once in the tunnel we start to descend the 1 in 330 grade towards Penge East. We pass through the station at 08.41 as our driver continues to accelerate to take advantage of the gradient which steepens to 1 in 110 as we emerge from the station. Heading inbound, a rake of Class 465 EMUs heads towards London. Kent House, with its two island platforms, is passed at 08.41; Kent House marks the bottom of the gradient from Penge and for the next mile and a half the train will be climbing with the maximum gradient (of 1 in 100) encountered just before Shortlands Junction and the summit of this short stretch. As we pass over the branch to Addiscombe the single-track Crystal Palace-Beckenham Junction line approaches from the south and the link to New Beckenham from the north. Immediately after passing through platform 3 at Beckenham Junction (08.42.30) an adverse signal forces our driver to brake slightly as an inbound EMU, formed of Class 466 No 466014 and Class 465 No 465025, heads back to Beckenham Junction. The signal was warning of the approach to Shortlands Junction, but fortunately this time we are not held.

At Shortlands Junction we are met by the line via Catford (see Chapter 10). The track arrangements at Shortlands station (passed at 08.44) mean that we traverse platform 2. We are now on a four-track section heading towards Bickley. From Shortlands station to Bickley Junction the gradient is 1 in 95 up

for most of the journey. We pass through Bromley South at 08.45.30 and then Bickley at 08.46.30. Again, as we approach a junction, the signals are against us and we decelerate in case we need to stop. Fortunately, as we reach Bickley Junction, we get a green and are able to take the chord from Bickley Junction to Petts Wood Junction. Although this chord existed before the arrival of international trains, it has been modified to accommodate Eurostar services. It is as we traverse this chord that control of the train passes from Victoria box to Ashford. An inbound EMU, with No 1613 bringing up the rear, rushes past in the up direction.

As we approach Petts Wood station we get the first indication of high-speed running when we pass a sign indicating 'HST90'; Eurostar services are treated as HSTs so are thus entitled to travel over this stretch at 90mph in contrast to normal services that are limited to 75mph. We pass through platform 2 at Petts Wood station on the down fast at 08.50.30. Whilst we are up front, in the passenger coaches French customs officers have started to undertake the passport checks; this will streamline arrival at Gare du Nord. On-board passport checks are undertaken on all services with the exception of those to Brussels, where the Belgian authorities have retained traditional passport checks in the station.

On the approach to Orpington we pass a 12-car EMU heading into London. Orpington is an important destination and its eight platforms and carriage sidings bear witness to the traffic that the station generates. Orpington was one of the stations that received attention in the build-up to the launch of Eurostar services, with international trains benefiting from investment in the new Kent Networker scheme. Two additional platforms, Nos 7 and 8, were constructed and two other platforms lengthened. This means that terminating trains, which used to utilise one

Left: With the Waterloo station throat in the background, TMST set No 3008 approaches Waterloo International on 22 July 1994 with a test train from Paris Gare du Nord. *Brian Morrison*

Below left: A dramatic panorama shows a busy scene at Waterloo on 1 February 1995 with Eurostar services to Brussels and Paris arriving and departing. Looking rather mundane in comparison, Class 423/1 No 3510 leaves the 'old' station with the 12.25 service to Farnham. Visible on the extreme left is the unique Scharfenburg coupling-fitted Class 73 with a Class 92 beyond. *Brian Morrison*

Above right: Heading along the bidirectionally-signalled line between International Junction and Nine Elms Junction — the Windsor Reversible Line — the 10.10 Waterloo International-Paris Gare du Nord services heads westwards shortly after its departure on 22 January 1995. The train is formed of sets Nos 3013 and 3014. *Brian Morrison*

Centre right: TMST sets Nos 3003 and 3004 head through Vauxhall *en route* to North Pole depot from Waterloo International on 14 February 1994. *Brian Morrison*

Below right: Access to the lines out of Victoria is gained via the Nine Elms flyover, which links Nine Elms Junction and Linford Street Junction. With Stewarts Lane depot to the centre left, the 12.12 Paris Gare du Nord-Waterloo International service makes its way past Factory Junction, Battersea, on 4 February 1995. The sweeping curve of the flyover and the length of the train can lead to dramatic views for passengers, particularly at night. *Brian Morrison*

Left: Heading for France, Eurostar Nos 3231 and 3232 pass Wandsworth Road station on 4 February 1995. Whilst the trains may be different, the backdrop, with Battersea Power Station on the right, will be familiar to generations of railway staff and enthusiasts. *Brian Morrison*

Below: The 10.28 Brussels-Midi-Waterloo International service passes a South London line Class 456 EMU at Wandsworth Road station on 1 June 1995. The TMST is formed of sets Nos 3205 leading and 3206. *Brian Morrison*

of the through platforms, can now use the new bays. Although the track from Petts Wood is cleared for 90mph running, it is rare for TMSTs to reach that speed and we have been averaging no more than 45mph as we pass through platform 3 at Orpington at 08.52. Immediately after Orpington the four-track section is reduced to two tracks before we reach Chelsfield (where the line limit is reduced to 80mph). Our speed is, however, still only 45mph as we amble through Chelsfield station at 08.53 and enter the 597yd-long Chelsfield Tunnel. We

are now starting to accelerate again and Knockholt station, which is shortly before the summit of the four-mile climb from Petts Wood Junction, is passed at 08.55 with the train travelling at just over 60mph. From the summit at Knockholt there is a four-mile descent until Dunton Green.

As we breast the summit at Knockholt an eight-car EMU heads back towards London. The train now enters the one mile 851yd-long Polhill Tunnel after which it emerges into open countryside. Our speed has again increased as we have descended from Knockholt and we pass through Dunton Green at 08.57.30. Dunton Green was, from 1881, the junction for the short branch to Westerham until its closure on 30 October 1961; there is little to indicate today the existence of this Kentish branch.

After a short level stretch at Dunton Green, the line ascends for a mile and a half to Sevenoaks. As we approach the station the line from Otford comes in from the east. We trundle through platform 2 at Sevenoaks — another station which was remodelled as part of the Kent Networker scheme with the aim of reducing conflicting movements from terminating trains — at 08.59.45 before entering the one mile 1,693yd-long Sevenoaks Tunnel which is on a falling 1 in 144 gradient. The speed limit through Sevenoaks is 70mph. One of the problems with running on the third-rail is that, unless the train is carefully driven, the gaps in the third-rail, which occur largely at junctions and stations, can cause the circuit breakers to trip out. There are five gaps in the third-rail in Sevenoaks Tunnel and our driver takes advantage of the downhill grade to avoid pushing the train too hard. Immediately after the tunnel the gradient increases to 1 in 122 and the maximum line speed is increased to 100mph. We pass through Hildenborough station at 09.03.30 with the train approaching the maximum line speed.

Left: Seen from the roof of an adjacent tower block, the 12.12 Paris Gare du Nord-Waterloo International service, formed of TMST sets Nos 3017 and 3018, passes Wandsworth Road station on 4 February 1995. *Brian Morrison*

Right: On 10 June 1995 the 10.23 Waterloo-Paris service was formed of TMST sets Nos 3015 (leading) and 3016. It is seen passing facelifted Class 4VEP No 3588 on a Dover Priory-Victoria service at Brixton. The lines in the foreground are used by Eurostar services to gain access to the Catford Loop. *Michael J. Collins*

Centre right: Pictured emerging from the tunnels at Penge East, the 12.23 Waterloo-Paris service heads out of London on 27 May 1995. The train is formed of sets Nos 3006 (leading) and 3005. *Michael J. Collins*

Below right: Pictured on a test run from North Pole depot to Dollands Moor on 23 November 1993, TMST set No 3103 passes Bromley South. *Brian Morrison*

As we approach Tonbridge the track levels out at the end of the six-mile descent from Sevenoaks and, before we enter Tonbridge station with its 75mph and 50mph speed limits over the curve and junction, our driver makes a slight brake application. Immediately prior to the junction at Tonbridge (at which the Redhill line comes in from the west) there are sidings to the south. An eight-car EMU heads away from Tonbridge back towards Sevenoaks. Tonbridge station is provided with four platform roads and two through lines and we carefully manoeuvre our way over the down fast through line at 09.06. As we pass through the station, a TMST heads towards London on the up fast. This is the late-running train No 9007, which was due to leave Paris at 07.10, but which is running behind schedule due to the effects of the strikes affecting the public sector (including the railways) in France at this time. Immediately after Tonbridge station as we head almost due east towards Paddock Wood, the line towards Hastings diverges southwards at Tonbridge East Junction. After Tonbridge station there is a slight

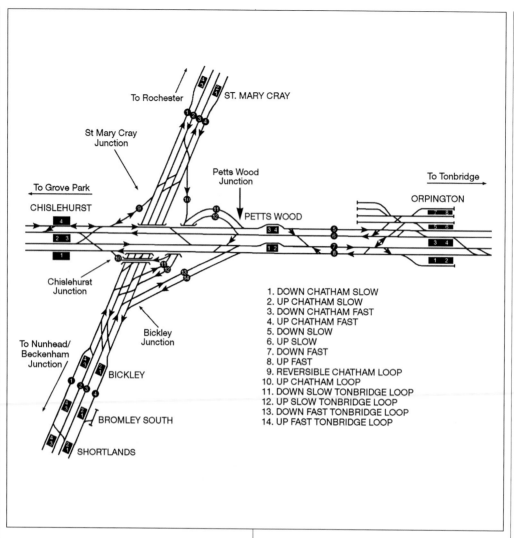

ST. MARY CRAY

St Mary Cray
Junction

Petts Wood
Junction

To Grove Park

To Tonbridge

CHISLEHURST

ORPINGTON

PETTS WOOD

Chislehurst
Junction

Bickley
Junction

To Nunhead/
Beckenham
Junction

BICKLEY

BROMLEY SOUTH

SHORTLANDS

1. DOWN CHATHAM SLOW
2. UP CHATHAM SLOW
3. DOWN CHATHAM FAST
4. UP CHATHAM FAST
5. DOWN SLOW
6. UP SLOW
7. DOWN FAST
8. UP FAST
9. REVERSIBLE CHATHAM LOOP
10. UP CHATHAM LOOP
11. DOWN SLOW TONBRIDGE LOOP
12. UP SLOW TONBRIDGE LOOP
13. DOWN FAST TONBRIDGE LOOP
14. UP FAST TONBRIDGE LOOP

uphill gradient for a mile and a half; the line speed limit increases to 90mph immediately after Tonbridge West Junction and to 100mph to the east of the station; however, these limits are academic as the train averages no more than 70mph between Tonbridge and Paddock Wood (09.10.30).

Paddock Wood is the junction for the line to Maidstone, which comes in from the north immediately after the station. The station is served by loops off the up and down fast lines and it is over the down fast that our train passes through. There is an

Above: The track arrangement at Bickley Junction; this was one of the locations on the English side where significant track alterations were undertaken to facilitate the operation of the Eurostar services. It is at this point that Eurostar trains pass from the control of Victoria IECC to that at Ashford.

eight-car EMU awaiting departure from the up platform (No 1). As we head out eastwards towards Headcorn, a Class 33 with an engineers' train heads inbound; it is, perhaps, a reflection of the decline of domestic freight traffic and locomotive-hauled trains generally that, on this particular occasion, this movement was the

Above: The 14.23 Waterloo-Paris service, formed of sets Nos 3214 (leading) and 3213, swings off the main line on to the Bickley Junction-Petts Wood Junction chord on 8 April 1996.
Brian Morrison

only active locomotive seen between London and the Channel Tunnel. Marden station is passed at 09.13.30 with our average speed now running at 90mph. A four-car EMU heads in the up direction; now that the morning peak is past, trains are reduced in length to off-peak requirements. Staplehurst station is passed at 09.15 followed by Headcorn at 09.17; our speed has now increased almost to the maximum of 100mph permitted over this section.

Headcorn was, until January 1954, the junction for the Kent & East Sussex Railway line southwards to Tenterden and Robertsbridge. K&ESR services ran from a bay platform on the southern side of the station. Evidence of the K&ESR survived until the construction of a new up freight loop in connection with the Channel Tunnel which obliterated the remaining traces. Quite what the late Col Stephens would make of the heavy freight trains

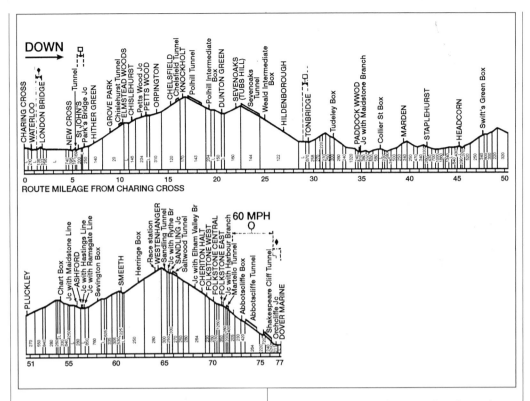

Gradient profile of the route from Petts Wood to Folkestone.

Above left: Passing Bickley Junction, the 14.27 Waterloo-Brussels service heads towards Petts Wood on 8 April 1996. The train was formed of sets Nos 3106 (leading) and 3105. The Bickley Junction-Petts Wood Junction chord is one of a number of sections of line upgraded to facilitate the introduction of Eurostar services. *Brian Morrison*

Left: With a track maintenance gang at work in the foreground, a London-bound Eurostar service (the 08.27 from Brussels), formed of Nos 3203 and 3204, heads towards London through the curve at Bickley Junction on 10 July 1996. *Brian Morrison*

Above: Gradient profile of the route from Petts Wood to Folkestone.

using the formation constructed for 'his' light railway is almost impossible to say! Headcorn station, like Paddock Wood, is served by loops off the through lines, and again we pass through on the down fast. Shortly after Headcorn we meet our second up TMST of the day; this is the 07.31 from Brussels, which again is running

slightly late due to the French industrial action.

Pluckley station is passed at 09.20.30 with the train running at 90mph. We are now on our approach to Ashford. At this time construction work at Ashford International is still incomplete, although the new domestic station is operational. Also at this time, Ashford station and its immediate vicinity are still under the control of Ashford panel before the completion of the Ashford IECC signalling scheme.

As we approach Ashford, Chart Leacon works appears on our right as our driver gently applies the brakes for our approach through Ashford B Junction, where the line from Maidstone approaches from the north. Situated in the domestic platforms are Class 411/5 EMU No 1611 and two DEMUs, Nos 202205 and 207203. We pass through the station on the down fast line at 09.25.15. To our left there is evidence of the continuing construction work on the

International platforms, which are due to come into operation in January 1996. The new — and very impressive — station was designed by Nick Derbyshire. It serves both domestic passengers (via a new concourse situated on the north side) and international travellers via a large block on the south. This block houses facilities for both arriving and departing passengers, including the customs hall. Segregated access to the new 400m-long International platforms is achieved by a footbridge. The scheme cost £100 million, half of which was funded by the construction company Laing as part of the government's Private Finance Initiative.

For our train, however, a stop at Ashford International is not yet on the timetable and so we pass through non-stop. Immediately to the south of the station the lines to Hastings and Canterbury head off south and north respectively. Our next point of interest comes almost immediately as the four tracks are reduced to two as we cross the (in)famous Willesborough Crossing with its manually-operated crossing gates. This location is regularly highlighted as emphasising the discrepancy between railway investment in France — where the LGV-Nord line was funded by the government — and Britain where the railways are trying to operate 21st century

Above: Seen from the rear, the 12.12 Paris Gare du Nord-Waterloo International service curves off the Petts Wood Junction-Bickley Junction chord on 25 March 1995 and joins the four-track main line towards London Victoria. The tracks in the foreground carry Victoria-Orpington local services. *Brian Morrison*

Above right: TMST sets Nos 3211 (leading) and 3212 approach Orpington on 30 January 1995 with the 12.53 Waterloo-Paris train. 'Networker' No 465020 is stabled in the sidings. *Brian Morrison*

Right: The 12.12 Paris-Waterloo service glides through Orpington in 30 January 1995. The train comprises sets Nos 3217 (leading) and 3218. *Brian Morrison*

equipment on 19th century infrastructure. Whether it is quaint or simply sad, our passengers speed past probably oblivious to the historical significance of the little crossing box that has just been passed.

The section from Ashford to the tunnel entrance is the only part of the route for which there is no alternative and thus each line is signalled for bidirectional use. There are, however, no problems today and our train is able to use the normal down line. Half a mile beyond Willesborough Crossing we pass back from Ashford panel's control to the Ashford IECC for the final stretch to Continental Junction. As we continue southwards we pass the freight terminal at

Sevington, which was constructed by Railfreight to receive the deliveries of construction material for use on the building of the tunnel. With construction work now completed, the loop, situated on the up line, and the sidings have rusted over.

We are now on the approach to the tunnel itself. There is little evidence now of the closed station at Smeeth, which lost its passenger services on 4 January 1954 and was closed completely on 18 April 1964, but just to the west of Westenhanger station are the disused platforms of Folkestone Racecourse station. Westenhanger station, one of the oldest on the line, opening originally on 7 February 1844 and known until 1874 as Westenhanger & Hythe, is passed at 09.34. A four-car EMU heads back towards London as our train enters the 100yd-long

Left: At a picturesque location between Knockholt and Dunton Green, TMST sets Nos 3101 (leading) and 3102 glide through the fields of Kent on a test run to Ashford and back on 11 February 1994. *Brian Morrison*

Below: On 7 February 1994 test train UK1 is seen at Polhill *en route* from North Pole International to Ashford. *Chris Wilson*

Right: The 12.31 Brussels-Waterloo Eurostar service approaches Dunton Green on 15 June 1997. The train is formed of Belgian sets Nos 3104 leading 3103. *Brian Morrison*

Below right: Ashford International. Eurostar services can approach the station with trains from London Waterloo via either the Tonbridge or Maidstone lines. The famous Willesborough box is situated immediately to the south of the four-track section through the station.

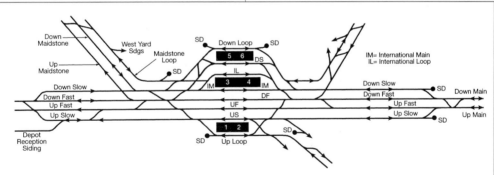

Sandling Tunnel. Sandling station is passed at 09.35; this was the junction for the line to Hythe and Sandgate and evidence of the platforms for the branch is visible to the right of the train. The branch opened through to Sandgate in October 1874; it was closed beyond Hythe in April 1931 and closed completely from Sandling to Hythe in December 1951.

It is as the train passes Sandling that passengers are given the first indication that the train is about to leave Britain, as an announcement — 'In a few minutes we shall be entering the Channel Tunnel. The journey time will be about 22 minutes. Please put your watches forward one hour.' — is made. This will be the last message made in English first; once French soil is reached the French language takes precedence.

Left: TMST sets Nos 3231 (leading) and 3232 work the 16.27 Waterloo International-Brussels-Midi train on 4 June 1995 as it approaches Sevenoaks. *Brian Morrison*

Centre left: On 30 July 1996 the 15.10 Paris Gare du Nord-Waterloo International service curves round on to CTR1 at Tonbridge. French sets Nos 3221 (leading) and 3222 head northwards towards Bickley Junction. *Brian Morrison*

Below : TMST sets Nos 3102 and 3101 glide through Paddock Wood station on 9 February 1994 on a test train from North Pole. *Brian Morrison*

Right: The 15.28 Brussels-Midi-Waterloo International service, formed of Nos 3218 (leading) and 3217, powers its way westwards between Staplehurst and Marden on 6 October 1996. The maximum speed permitted for TMST sets in Britain is no more than 160km/h (100mph), a sorry contrast to the 300km/h (186mph) allowed on the high-speed lines in Europe.
Brian Morrison

Centre right: Having just passed through Ashford, the 13.04 Paris Gare du Nord-Waterloo service heads westwards along the old SECR main line towards Tonbridge at Pluckley on 6 October 1996. The train is formed of North Pole-allocated Nos 3018 (leading) and 3017.
Brian Morrison

Below: Heading for Lille and Brussels, the 12.27 service from Waterloo, formed of Nos 3224 (leading) and 3223, approaches Ashford on 28 January 1995.
Brian Morrison

Left: With construction work proceeding apace at the new Ashford International station, the 11.27 Waterloo-Brussels-Midi service, formed of TMST sets Nos 3008 and 3007, passes through Ashford on 13 October 1995. *Brian Morrison*

Below left: Passing Ashford on the through down line, with evidence of the now nearly complete International platform behind it, the 13.57 service from Waterloo to Paris, formed of Nos 3104 (leading) and 3103, rushes towards the Channel Tunnel on 14 July 1996.

Above right: TMST sets Nos 3220 and 3221 pass the old Ashford Works on 28 January 1995, forming the 12.53 Waterloo-Paris service. *Brian Morrison*

Centre right: Formed of Class 207/2 DEMU No 207203, the 12.22 'Marsh Line' service for Hastings awaits departure from Ashford on 13 October 1995 as the 11.23 Waterloo-Paris Eurostar service passes through on the down main. The train was formed of units Nos 3107 and 3108. The International platforms are located on the right of the picture, with the glass-enclosed footbridge giving access to the International station facilities. *Brian Morrison*

Below right: A location that is often portrayed to highlight the anachronisms of high-speed railway operation in Britain and to draw attention to the disparity in current investment between Britain and France over the fast links to the Channel is Willesborough level crossing. This manually-operated crossing is situated just to the south of Ashford and emphasising the contrast between 19th and late 20th century technology, TMST sets Nos 3207 and 3208 pass the diminutive box on 13 October 1995 with the 14.16 service from Paris to Waterloo. *Brian Morrison*

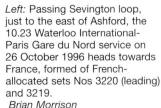

Left: Passing Sevington loop, just to the east of Ashford, the 10.23 Waterloo International-Paris Gare du Nord service on 26 October 1996 heads towards France, formed of French-allocated sets Nos 3220 (leading) and 3219.
Brian Morrison

Centre left: In order to facilitate the construction of the Channel Tunnel a new freight terminal was established at Sevington, just south of Ashford, to receive construction materials. With the construction work now completed, these sidings remain but are now disused. On 15 August 1996 the 18.27 service from Waterloo to Brussels, formed of TMST sets Nos 3105/3106, passes the gated entrance to the Sevington yard. *Brian Morrison*

Below left: Passing the seemingly abandoned old station building at Westenhanger, TMST sets No 3221 and 3222 provide an ancient and modern comparison on 2 March 1996 as the 14.23 service from London to Paris heads towards the Channel Tunnel. *Brian Morrison*

Above right: The 13.07 Paris-Waterloo service is pictured near Westenhanger on 2 March 1996. The train is formed of sets Nos 3216 (leading) and 3215.
Brian Morrison

Right: The last train of the day to Brussels-Midi, the 18.27 from Waterloo International, threads a path through the Kent countryside between Westenhanger and Sandling on 13 June 1996. The train is formed of Nos 3001 and 3002. It is as the train travels towards Sandling that passengers are alerted to the fact that it is about to enter the Channel Tunnel and the driver makes preparations for the first change of power supply.
Brian Morrison

Through the Tunnel to France

As the train passes through Sandling Tunnel the driver starts to make preparations for the change from Britain's third-rail system to the 25kV configuration appropriate for the Channel Tunnel. There are two selector switches in the cab: one controls the position of the pick-up gear and the second controls the type of current supply. In order to start the reconfiguration, our driver turns the pick-up switch to '0', which has the effect of retracting the pick-up shoes used on the third rail. The train is now coasting and will continue to do so for a short distance of some two miles through Sandling station itself (09.35) and the 954yd-long Saltwood Tunnel. As we approach the end of this section, the driver moves the current supply switch to 'ET' (Eurotunnel) and engages 'N' on the pick-up switch. This has the effect of raising the pantograph to the appropriate height for the Channel Tunnel. There are two other consequences of this action. Firstly, the speedometer display now reads in km/h rather than in the mph that was used through England and secondly the clock automatically switches to European time — none of the manual changes here that the passengers will have to undertake.

Left: On 7 July 1994 TMST sets Nos 3101 and 3102 await departure from Waterloo International with a test train to Dollands Moor. *Brian Morrison*

The passengers, comfortably seated, will be unaware of these changes. Rather, they will be conscious of the expanse of the new Dollands Moor freight terminal situated to the north of the line, with its rakes of wagons and stabled Class 92 electrics and Class 47 diesel-electrics awaiting their next turns. As our train heads towards the tunnel, an inbound Eurostar service is emerging from the Eurotunnel complex onto the Railtrack lines towards Ashford. At Continental Junction (09.36.30) our train passes from the control of Ashford box to that of Eurotunnel's Folkestone control room. The scale of Eurotunnel's Cheriton complex is apparent as our train passes over the arrival lines for the car and freight shuttle services. To the south of the running lines are Eurotunnel's maintenance sidings and shuttle storage sidings; the eagle-eyed or the railway enthusiast may be able to catch a glimpse of the diesel locomotives owned by Eurotunnel for use in the Channel Tunnel when the power has been disconnected. These locomotives are fitted with equipment to retain the exhaust and thus to the casual viewer look akin to the heads and shoulders of Cybermen from 'Doctor Who' when seen from the side. To the north of the running lines are the loading platforms for the passenger and freight shuttles.

At 09.38 our train enters the tunnel. In

Left: Although Dollands Moor International is primarily a freight yard, it can also be used for the storage of TMST sets as here, on 3 August 1995, when the 11.57 Waterloo-Paris service was photographed passing the yard. *Brian Morrison*

Left: TMST sets Nos 3101 and 3102 depart from Dollands Moor with a crew-training trip to Waterloo International and North Pole on 17 June 1994. The single-road shed to the left of the train is the locomotive repair shed. Visible in the otherwise deserted yard is a Class 47. Access to each of the freight yard roads is via ramps and these can be seen to the left of the rear power car of the departing TMST. *Chris Wilson*

Right: Probably a 'dangerous load' (the second vehicle carries a 'no entry' sign on the wagon side), this unlikely train passes Dollands Moor at Continental Junction on 12 April 1995 heading towards London. The locomotives are Class 47/0s, with (appropriately) No 47053 *Dollands Moor International* leading No 47228. In Dollands Moor Yard can be seen a Brussels-Waterloo Eurostar service diverted through the freight yard because of problems with the preceding service from Paris blocking the main line at this point. *Brian Morrison*

order to fulfil Eurotunnel's operating requirements and in the event of an emergency, when the train could be reversed out of the tunnel, a second qualified member of the train crew is positioned in the rear power car whilst the train is in transit over Eurotunnel metals. So far as Eurotunnel is concerned, the company's metals are divided into four signalling areas: '12' covers the Cheriton terminal; '13' cover the Coquelles terminal; whilst '14' and '15' cover the down and up tunnels respectively. Each tunnel is bidirectionally signalled and, with the use of the two intermediate crossovers (situated roughly one-third and two-thirds of the way through the tunnel), allows considerable flexibility of operation. The crossovers were

designed to allow a section of the tunnel to be closed for routine maintenance whilst still permitting a near normal service to operate. In the event, the flexibility was to be of immense use after the fire in November 1996, when one section of the tunnel was out of action for 8 months for repair.

Much has been written about the construction of the tunnel elsewhere; here it suffices to note a certain amount of information pertaining to the tunnel's nature and its impact on operation. Each bore of the two running tunnels is 27ft in diameter. The tightest curves have a radius of 4.2km and the maximum speed in the tunnel is 160km/h (100mph). Train control in the tunnel is undertaken by use of the French

TVM430, which cuts in as the train enters Eurotunnel property. There are km posts every 100m within the tunnel; km post 10 is at the British portal whilst km post 60.5 is situated at the French end. From the British portal the train descends a gradient of 1 in 90. In order to avoid the strobe effect from lighting in the tunnel, which might have disorientated a driver, the TMST sets are designed with no side cab windows and with the driver sitting centrally in the cab. There are pictograms on the tunnel walls to indicate the gradients. During periods of maintenance there is increased lighting in the tunnel; apart from its own 'Le Shuttle' locomotives Eurotunnel also owns a number of diesel locomotives for use with this work. There are five locomotives designated as rescue locomotives for use in the event of a train failure and 10 maintenance locomotives (constructed by Krupp-Mak).

In terms of the tunnel, each bore extends approximately 38km below the sea bed and the sea bed is a minimum of 45m and a maximum of 75m above the tunnel roof. Without some form of cooling system, the tunnel's heat would rapidly exceed the normal operating temperature of 25-35° Celcius.

To the passengers, however, the tunnel is no more than a 20min loss of daylight; whilst they may appreciate the technological triumph represented by the construction of the tunnel, it is very difficult to get a full appreciation of the scope of the work through the carriage windows.

Far left: Awaiting a train to take through the Channel Tunnel, SNCF Class 22xxx locomotives Nos 22380 and 22402 *Saint-Die Des Vosges* are seen in Dollands Moor Yard on 14 June 1994 alongside TMST sets Nos 3007 and 3008, which had arrived on a test train from North Pole. *Brian Morrison*

Below left: Designed for Channel Tunnel freight traffic, the Class 92s are designed to operate both under the 25kV catenary and on the third-rail. Two of the class, Nos 92016 *Brahms* and 92028 *Saint-Saens*, are seen at Dollands Moor on 13 October 1995. *Brian Morrison*

Right: Traversing the reception loop at Cheriton, having travelled through the Channel Tunnel, 'Le Shuttle', with Bo-Bo-Bo No 9023 at the rear, arrives from Coquelles with a lorry train on 14 June 1994. The rake was headed by sister locomotive No 9003. *Brian Morrison*

Below: On 11 March 1995 TMST sets Nos 3005 and 3006 pass through Continental Junction with the 06.57 service from Waterloo to Brussels. It is at this point that the train shifts from 750V dc to 25kV ac power supply. The Railtrack route to Folkestone heads off to the right. On the extreme left can be seen a further SNCF Class 22xxx electric

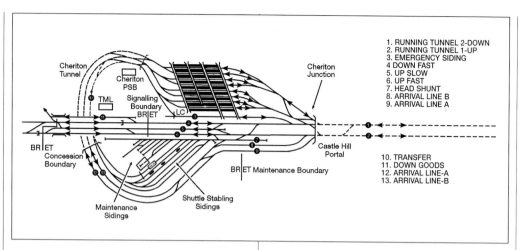

1. RUNNING TUNNEL 2-DOWN
2. RUNNING TUNNEL 1-UP
3. EMERGENCY SIDING
4. DOWN FAST
5. UP SLOW
6. UP FAST
7. HEAD SHUNT
8. ARRIVAL LINE B
9. ARRIVAL LINE A

10. TRANSFER
11. DOWN GOODS
12. ARRIVAL LINE-A
13. ARRIVAL LINE-B

Above: The huge Eurotunnel complex at Cheriton handles not only Eurostar and conventional freight traffic, but also the car and lorry shuttle services. There are also sidings provided for the maintenance trains.

Below: With another Eurostar on test behind the fence at Dollands Moor International yard, together with two Class 92s, the 15.19 Paris Nord-Waterloo International service passes onto the Railtrack main line at Continental Junction on 3 August 1995. The train is formed of Nos 3216 and 3215. *Brian Morrison*

Right: The sheer scale of the Eurotunnel site at Cheriton can be appreciated in this superb view taken from above the portals of the tunnel itself as the 16.27 Waterloo-Brussels service heads towards Europe on 3 August 1995. On the right can be seen the Eurotunnel shuttle facility, whilst the company's maintenance facility can be seen in the left background. *Brian Morrison*

Through France to Paris

Following a couple of slight brake applications as our driver responds to the instructions from the TVM430, our train emerges up the 1 in 91 gradient towards daylight and the French portal at Beussingues (km post 116 — distances from this point are noted against the km post 0, which is situated 10km southeast of Lille where the high-speed line towards Calais diverges from the new line to Brussels) at 09.59 and climbs towards the station. The Coquelles terminal of Eurotunnel is to the north of the line towards Lille, alongside the conventional SNCF route linking Calais-Fréthun with Calais-Ville. The complicated track arrangements at this point are illustrated by the adjacent diagram (see page 77). The train passes from Eurotunnel to SNCF control as it negotiates the crossovers immediately to the east of the Beussingues portal. As we emerge from the tunnel one of Eurotunnel's freight shuttles enters the second bore heading back towards Britain.

Above left: The complex network of lines at the French end of the Channel Tunnel is evident on 7 April 1995 as French-owned TMST Nos 3264/3213 emerges from the tunnel mouth into Beussingues Cutting with the 12.53 service from Waterloo to Paris Gare du Nord. *Chris Wilson*

Left: TMST sets Nos 3013 and 3014, working the 12.53 service from Waterloo to Paris, depart from Calais-Fréthun on 4 February 1995, having made an additional stop at the station. *Chris Wilson*

On emerging from the tunnel, our driver has once again to reconfigure the pantographs, this time to the standard required for the normal French 25kV. The switch controlling the pick-ups is moved to '0', thereby retracting the pantographs before the current selector switch is turned to 'F' for the French system. This achieved, the pick-up switch is turned to 'N'. Calais-Fréthun station is on two levels. The upper levels serve the Eurostar services, whilst at the lower level there are platforms handling the traditional (but now electrified) SNCF route from Calais to Boulogne.

The station at Calais-Fréthun is passed at 11.00 French time (10.00 UK time; remember the clocks have to go forward an hour!). Both before and after the train passes the station our driver is accelerating. The journey between Calais and Paris is one which, in theory, looks simple but which requires considerable skill on the part of the driver. Taking advantage of the high power to weight ratio of both the TGVs and the TMSTs, the track alignment of the LGV-Nord is relatively highly graded and the driver will need to make sensible use of the controls to ensure that the maximum speed permitted by the TVM430 is maintained and that the passengers don't experience any unnecessary acceleration or deceleration; it is worth, however, recalling here that the

Left: Heading towards the Channel, French-owned TMST sets Nos 3210/3209 pass near the village of Watterdam, between Lille and Calais, on 12 August 1997 with the 09.10 Paris Gare du Nord-Waterloo service. *Colin J. Marsden*

Centre left: One of the Belgian-owned TMST rakes, Nos 3102/3101, is recorded at Watterdam on 12 August 1997 whilst forming the 09.10 Waterloo-Paris Marne-la-Valle/Chessy service. This, incidentally, was the first set to be commissioned for Anglo-French running. *Colin J. Marsden*

Below: An interesting contrast in front end design was displayed at Lille-Flandres station on 5 October 1995 in connection with the Eurailspeed conference. Closest to the camera is TMST set No 3201. In the middle is AVE TGV No 16 (owned by the Spanish State Railways RENFE), whilst on the right is one of the ICE units (Nos 410 052/552) of DB (German State Railways). *Brian Morrison*

TMST set has a lower power output than the TGV-Nord sets that also operate over the route. A further change of configuration is required at this point to switch the power supply from the standard French 25kV to the fixed overhead of the LGV line; again our driver switches the pick-ups to '0' before turning the current selector switch to 'GV' for the LGV and then re-engaging the pantographs. Our train passes the 100km post at 11.05.30. The LGV-Nord is designed for bi-directional running, but on this occasion our train will be taking the left-hand running line.

Acceleration of the train is rapid and we soon reach the maximum speed of 300km/h. It is an instruction that drivers are to alert the train crew when the maximum speed is about to be attained and so our driver makes use of the train phone to tell the Train Manager that this milestone is about to be achieved. The Train Manager makes an announcement to the passengers — the first that will be in French rather than in English — to the effect that the train is now travelling at its maximum permitted speed. Safely cocooned in their coaches, most passengers will be scarcely aware of the rapidly passing French

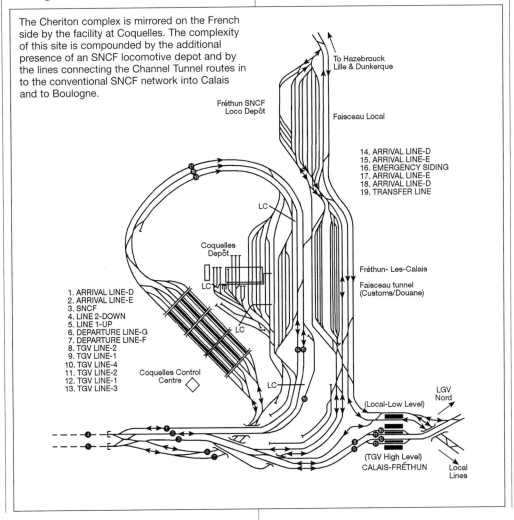

The Cheriton complex is mirrored on the French side by the facility at Coquelles. The complexity of this site is compounded by the additional presence of an SNCF locomotive depot and by the lines connecting the Channel Tunnel routes in to the conventional SNCF network into Calais and to Boulogne.

Fréthun SNCF Loco Depôt

To Hazebrouck Lille & Dunkerque

Faisceau Local

14. ARRIVAL LINE-D
15. ARRIVAL LINE-E
16. EMERGENCY SIDING
17. ARRIVAL LINE-E
18. ARRIVAL LINE-D
19. TRANSFER LINE

LC

Coquelles Depôt

Fréthun- Les-Calais

Faisceau tunnel (Customs/Douane)

1. ARRIVAL LINE-D
2. ARRIVAL LINE-E
3. SNCF
4. LINE 2-DOWN
5. LINE 1-UP
6. DEPARTURE LINE-G
7. DEPARTURE LINE-F
8. TGV LINE-2
9. TGV LINE-1
10. TGV LINE-4
11. TGV LINE-2
12. TGV LINE-1
13. TGV LINE-3

Coquelles Control Centre

LGV Nord

(Local-Low Level)

(TGV High Level) CALAIS-FRÉTHUN

Local Lines

Left: Apart from Paris Gare du Nord, Eurostar services also provide a link to the Eurodisney complex. Here, pictured at Gevrelle, just to the south of Lille, on 12 July 1996, is the 18.35 service from Marne-la-Vallé/Chessy (Eurodisney) to London Waterloo formed of TMST Nos 3219/3220. *Colin J. Marsden*

Centre left: Evidence of the once-thriving coal industry of the region is all too clear in the background as TMST Nos 3205/3206 passes Dourges on the LGV-Nord with the 08.13 Paris Gare du Nord-Waterloo service on 12 July 1996. *Chris Wilson*

Below left: TMST Nos 3010/3009 pass Beaumont, near Lille, on 11 July 1996 with the 18.35 Paris Marne la Vallé/Chessy service to Waterloo. In the background can be seen the A1 motorway. *Colin J. Marsden*

Right: Eurostar sets Nos 3206 and 3205 speed past at 300km/h on the LGV-Nord line near Rouex on a test run from Le Landy to Lille-Flandres on 10 March 1994. The spur coming in from the right links the LGV with the conventional line from Arras to Douai. *Chris Wilson*

landscape; only our driver, with his eye firmly attuned to the TVM430, will be fully conscious of the speed.

The first major engineering work to be encountered — at km post 81 — is the Haute Colme Viaduct which is 1,827m long. This viaduct crosses over the traditional SNCF route from Hazebrouck to Calais — which was electrified on 15 June 1993 and completed the electrification of the 'classic' route from Calais — as well as the River Aa and the Haute Colme Canal. Much of the traditional infrastructure in this region was funded through a FFr519 million (£50 million) scheme between SNCF, the regional council and central government; this work included the spur at Cassel (see below) as well as the electrification of the Boulogne-Calais, Lille-Baisieux and Douai-Cambrai lines. Our journey continues to be governed by the reading on the TVM430; km post 75 is passed at 10.11.10. The next excitement is just to the south of Cassel, where the electrified Dunkerque-Hazebrouck line passes under the high-speed line. A connection coming in from the north provides access to the LGV-Nord for trains to and from Dunkerque. Immediately after this point, at km post 62, the Eurostar train passes the site of the LGV-Nord construction site at Oxelaëre. This was one of three construction sites established for the building of the LGV-Nord.

Km post 60 is passed at 10.14.15 and post 45 at 10.17.20. At km post 42 the electrified line between Lille and Hazebrouck. The 40km post is passed at 10.18.20 before the freight-only line between Armentières (to the north) and Merville passes below us. Km post 30 is met at 10.20.30 and the train is now on the approach to Lille. The TVM430 comes into play, telling the driver to decelerate. He gently eases the controller back engaging the brakes to bring the train to the required

Left: On 11 July 1996 TMST sets Nos 3229/3230 travel at line speed on one of the downhill sections of the LGV-Nord at Rouex with the 11.43 Paris Gare du Nord-Waterloo service. *Colin J. Marsden*

Below: Eurostar (UK) Ltd TMST sets Nos 3016/3015 pass Croisilles Junction, to the south of Rouex, where the Paris-Arras high-speed line diverges from the TGV-Nord line towards Lille, with the 11.57 Waterloo-Paris Gare du Nord service on 11 July 1996. The steep gradient of the LGV-Nord line passing over the Arras line is evident in this view. *Colin J. Marsden*

Right: A diagrammatic representation of the LGV-Nord from Calais to the northern outskirts of Paris.

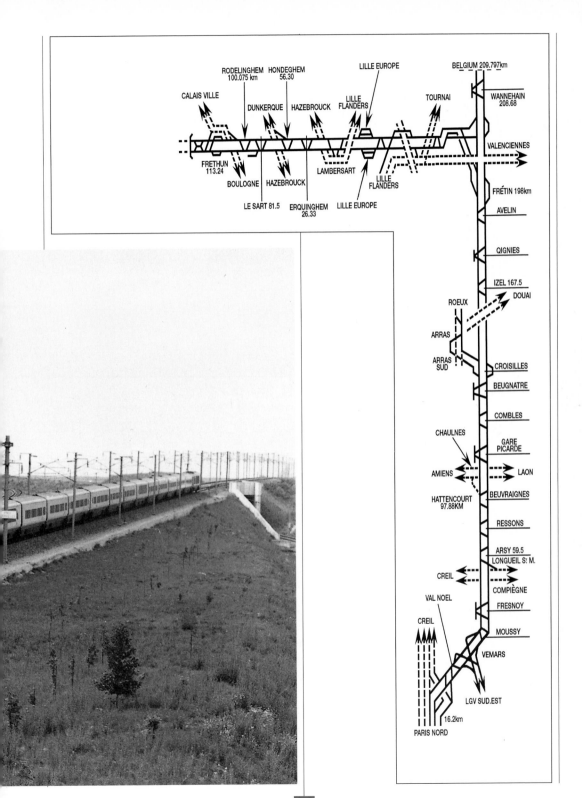

speed. We pass the 20km post at 10.23.20 before our train makes a sharp ascent and descent over the Lille-Hazebrouck line as both routes approach Lille proper. The LGV-Nord runs parallel and to the north of the conventional line at this point and there are crossovers provided to allow access between the two routes. Immediately after the station of Lambersart on the conventional line, the traditional route crosses over the LGV-Nord as it heads to join the route in from Roubaix before reaching Lille-Flandres station.

Having diverged from the conventional line, our train enters a two-kilometre tunnel under Lille; it is on this stretch that Lille-Europe station is being completed, although our train is not timetabled to stop. We pass through the platforms of the new station at 10.26. Lille-Europe station is provided with three pairs of tracks. The central pair of these lack platforms and are designed for the use of non-stop London-Paris trains, which will negotiate these lines at 200km/h (125mph) and it is over these

Above: Pictured at Dourges, just to the south of Arras on the LGV-Nord, on 12 July 1996, the 04.53 service from London Waterloo to Paris Gare du Nord heads south alongside, again, the A1 motorway. At this point TMST sets travel at around 290km/h. *Colin J. Marsden*

lines that our driver has taken the train through the station. To either side of these tracks is an island platform, providing the station with four platform faces (Nos 43-46; the numbering of these platforms is explained by the requirements of the local signalling system). These platforms are used by TGV services to Dunkerque, Calais and Boulogne, as well as by stopping Eurostar services. The TGV services from Paris to Lille still use the old Lille-Flandres station, which is situated about 400m to the south.

The construction of Lille-Europe station, with its links into the city's automated VAL metro and conventional Mongy tramway, has been the focus of a major redevelopment of this part of Lille; again much of this redevelopment will be peripheral to the passengers' view as the train traverses the station, but it is indicative of the level of investment that has gone into SNCF as part of the Channel Tunnel scheme.

Emerging again into daylight, the high-speed line is immediately crossed overhead by the conventional line that heads towards Roubaix and Mouscron. At this point the LGV-Nord runs parallel with the conventional SNCF line towards Paris. The conventional line towards Baisieux heads eastwards at this point; there are connections between the LGV-Nord and classic line here, which allowed (until the opening of the new Belgian high-speed line in 1997) access for Eurostar services to Brussels (see next chapter). As our driver accelerates away from Lille (the maximum for the stretch from this point to the southern junction at Fretin is 220km/h or 137.5mph), the station of Mont-de-Terre is passed on the conventional lines. The time is now 11.28.40. Our train is heading southeastwards towards the junction at Fretin. This triangular junction (with flyovers) sees the then still unused link to the Belgian high-speed line head southeastwards as our train takes the more southerly route towards Paris. The Paris-Brussels spur comes in from the east (11.30); at this time the line is still incomplete and there is evidence of the construction work. Immediately before the southernmost part of the junction, the classic Lille-Valenciennes line passes over the LGV-Nord.

Distances are now recorded from the point (Villiers-le-bel-Gonesse), just to the north of Paris, where the LGV-Nord diverges from the classic Paris-Amiens line. At this point we are at km post 198. We pass the 190 km post at 11.32 as a northbound TMST heads towards Lille. From about 185km from the outskirts and for about 130km thereafter, the LGV-Nord parallels the French A1 motorway. As our train hurtles southwards, it appears as though the cars on the adjacent road are stationary; in reality they are permitted to travel at more than 100km/h, but this means that they will still take twice as long to reach the outskirts of Paris as the train. Km post 180 is passed at 11.34.15; the last 10km have taken precisely 2min 15 sec and our speed is currently 265km/h (166mph); although the maximum line speed is 300km/h, if the train is running to time or early then there is no need to use the maximum speed permitted. Our driver continues at 265km/h, passing km post 170 at 11.36.30. A link at km post 162 comes in from the west; this provides access to the Arras-Valenciennes line, which passes under the LGV-Nord almost immediately thereafter.

Although it will have been imperceptible to the passengers, our driver has, over the past few kilometres, been gently accelerating, with the result that km post 160 is passed at 11.38.35, the train's speed having increased to 285km/h (175mph). This speed is maintained through to km post 150 (11.40.40) and 140 (11.42.45). At km post 147 a further spur heads westwards from *Bif Croisilles*; this provides access to the classic route from Douai to Arras and this, in conjunction with the spur further north, will allow TGVs to serve Arras. When the LGV-Nord was first opened, the link from Croisilles north to Lille was not complete, due to earlier opposition to the line's construction from residents at Seclin, and this section did not open until three months after the remainder of the line from Paris.

The speed of 285km/h is maintained through km posts 130 (11.44.50) and 120 (11.46.55) before the site of Gare Picarde is passed. This station represents one of the most controversial aspects of the whole LGV-Nord project. In a demonstration of forward planning, SNCF decided to construct a station at this point, rather than

some six kilometres further south at the point where the LGV-Nord passes over the Amiens-Chaulnes-Mennessis line (and thus provided an interchange with the lines serving the district's major towns), to serve both the existing A1 motorway and a proposed major road linking St-Quentin with Amiens. Despite the opposition of the local population, the government sided with SNCF and the new station serves, primarily, TGV services that bypass Paris.

Km post 110 is passed at 11.49.00, with the train still travelling at 285km/h. Following a slight deceleration to 265km/h the 100km post is passed at 11.51.15 after which the train again accelerates slightly back to 285km/h. Just to the south of the 100km post, the LGV-Nord passes over the non-electrified passenger line from Amiens to Mennessis; immediately to the east of the LGV-Nord a freight only branch diverges from the conventional line to head north towards Péronne and Roisel. A single

track link from the west is provided at this point to a junction at Chaulnes. Shortly after this junction the line passes over the short freight-only line that links Chaulnes with Roye. The 90km post is passed at 11.53.20; the 80km post is met at 11.55.25 and km post 70 a further 2min 5sec later at 11.57.30.

At km post 62, the LGV-Nord passes over the non-electrified line from Amiens via Montdidier to Compiègne. The 60km post is passed at 11.59.40, with the train now travelling at 260km/h. Just to the south of this point the LGV-Nord crosses over the electrified line from Creil to Compiègne and a spur from this line links up with the LGV-Nord from the east. The third of the three construction sites — at Longueil-Sainte-Marie — was situated here; this is the only one of the trio to be retained in part for maintenance of the route. Acceleration back to 285km/h sees the train pass the 50km post at 12.01.05

Left: TMST set No 3221 hurries through Saint Denis station on the outskirts of Paris with the 15.19 service from Paris to Waterloo on 29 January 1996. *Colin J. Marsden*

Above: Heading into Paris on the final leg of its three-hour journey from Waterloo, TMST sets Nos 3012/3011 pass through Saint Denis with the 11.57 service on 29 January 1996. *Colin J. Marsden*

Centre right: TMST set No 3205 arrives at Paris Gare du Nord prior to running a service to Waterloo International. Note the Metro train on the bridge overhead. *Colin J. Marsden*

Right: TMST set No 3205 stands at the buffer stops at Gare du Nord with a TGV rake on the right. *Colin J. Marsden*

and the 45km post at 12.02.50.

As we pass the 45km post the TVM430 indicates that we need to reduce our speed and the driver eases back on the controller so that we are travelling at 210km/h (130mph) by km post 40 (12.04.15). It is clear by now that we are following a slower-moving train into Paris as the TVM430 demands a further reduction of speed. Again our driver eases back on the controller to reduce speed, with the result that we pass km post 35 travelling at 190km/h (120mph) at 12.05.50. The train continues to decelerate slightly, taking the speed down to 180km/h (112mph) at km post 30, to 157km/h (98mph) at km post 25 and to 150km/h (94mph) at km post 20. As we head into Paris so a northbound TGV heads in the opposite direction. At km post 15, by which time our speed has been reduced to 145km/h (91mph), we traverse the triangular junction at Moussy-le-Neuf. It is at this point that the LGV-Interconnexion deviates from the LGV-Nord. This line, which opened in mid-1994, runs to the east

Above: A general view of the International platforms at Gare du Nord with TMST set No 3205 standing in the station on 13 April 1994. The International platforms are separated from the main concourse by a simple glass screen — a considerable contrast to the facilities at Waterloo. The Eurostar departures area is situated on a mezzanine floor visible on the left of the photograph; access for departing passengers to the platforms is gained by the footbridge.
Colin J. Marsden

of Paris and provides a route by which inter-regional TGV services can operate without having to use central Paris. The first station on the LGV-Interconnexion heading southwards from this point is Roissy/Aéroport Charles de Gaulle, which serves one of Paris's international airports as well as the Disneyland complex; this station is served by one return working by Eurostar each day from London Waterloo.

Normally, it is at this point that the Eurostar services would start to decelerate gradually before arriving at the junction with the original main line at Villiers-le-bel-Gonesse, but because of the earlier brake applications our speed has already been much reduced. This process continues with the speedometer reading only 124km/h (75mph) as we reach km post 5. It is at this point that our driver, for the last time on this journey, renconfigures the pantograph, this time from LGV to conventional 25kV operation. The line, on the approach to the flyover junction at Villiers-le-bel Gonesse- also comes under the control of conventional colour light signalling.

The LGV-Nord joins the conventional SNCF route north of Paris 16.2km from the city. A further slight brake application sees the train at the junction (12.19.00) travelling at 130km/h (80mph). Immediately south of the complex junction is the station of Villiers-le-bel-Gonesse. Following the junction our driver has been able to apply a bit more power, with the result that our train next passes the station at Garges (12.20.35) travelling at 150km/h (94mph). This increase is, however, only temporary, as a further brake application just south of Garges station, on the approach to the junction at Pierrefitte-Stains, where a spur links eastwards into the freight-only line from Sartrouville to Noisy (which passes over the line into Paris Gare du Nord). Pierrefitte-Stains station is passed at 12.21.50, with the train now running at 100km/h (63mph).

On the approaches to the junction north of Saint Denis an SNCF double-deck EMU No 20517 (one of the Class Z20500 units) heads northbound. Immediately to the north of the junction our train passes the depot of Les Joncherolles; this new facility handles many of the locomotives and units used on the northern suburban services. Normally Eurostar services would approach the junction at Saint-Denis travelling at about 120km/h (75mph), but we have been running at less than that speed for some time. To the north of Saint-Denis station, the line towards Persan-Beaumont comes in from the west. Saint-Denis station

is passed at 11.25.40 with our speed now no more than 60km/h (37mph).

The train passes the shed at Saint-Denis (situated on the west side of the running lines) before passing under two overbridges; the second of these (which carries the A86 motorway) is the point at which the TGVs and TMSTs use the newly-built dive-under which transfers the fast lines from the eastern to the western approaches to Gare du Nord and thus to the dedicated platforms in the station. We emerge back into daylight midway along the northernmost part of the Le Landy complex.

Le Landy depot is a pivotal establishment for SNCF's involvement with Eurostar as well as for its operations over the LGV-Nord line and for the Thalys services to Brussels and Amsterdam. The first depot at Le Landy was opened in 1878 by the Compagnie des Chemins de Fer du Nord and initially covered seven hectares. The modern depot covers 30 hectares, of which some 38,600sq m are covered. There are three distinct elements to the depot complex, all of which are visible from the train. The northernmost facility is Le Landy Pleyel. This establishment, with repair, preparation and examination sheds, deals with the coaching stock of the LGV-Nord TGVs. Of primary interest, so far as this book is concerned, is Le Landy Centre. This facility was completely rebuilt in 1992 to handle the rakes of stock used on both Eurostar and Thalys services. Accommodation provided at Le Landy Centre includes the three-road *Bâtiment Transmanche* (Channel Tunnel Building), which is 400m long, the eight-road *Bâtiment Continental* (Continental Building), which is 200m long, and the *Bâtiment Crgo (chantier de remplacement des gros organs* — the heavy repair workshop, where major overhauls can be undertaken). As at North Pole, Le Landy Centre is designed to be able to test all the different voltage and power equipment settings. The third element at

Right: Eurostar sets are serviced at Le Landy depot in Paris. This facility, which is shared with the French TGV-Nord sets and those units used on the Thalys services to Brussels and Amsterdam, is located just to the north of Gare du Nord. Providing a contrast in front ends on 11 June 1996 — and a reflection of the photographer — are TGV-R No 4504, TMST No 3205 and TGV-Thalys No 4341.
Colin J. Marsden

Le Landy, Le Landy Sud, handles the reception and dispatch of rolling stock. Apart from the 16 rakes of TMSTs allocated to SNCF and all based at Le Landy, the depot is also home to 10 rakes of three-current Thalys stock and six rakes of four-current Thalys stock as well as 50 dual-current TGVs and 30 three-current TGVs. It all makes for an impressive installation immediately to the north of Gare du Nord.

We arrive in Paris Gare du Nord at 12.30.55; the reason for our slightly tardy journey into Paris over the southern end of the LGV-Nord becomes apparent, as an earlier service has only just arrived in front of us. Our train draws up to the buffer stops in platform No 4. Unlike both Waterloo and Brussels-Midi, where new facilities have been provided, the Eurostar platforms at Paris Gare du Nord have been converted (and lengthened) from existing platforms. Although there is a physical barrier between the Eurostar section of the station and the remainder, this is only a glass screen separating the arriving passengers from the main station concourse; this helps to make Eurostar services arriving in Paris seem much more 'domestic' than arrivals in either London or Brussels.

For our arriving passengers, detraining takes a few minutes and then there is the onward journey into Paris itself. Given the arrival time, most passengers will probably be thinking about lunch. Unlike the passengers, however, the unit will be prepared to make an almost immediate return northwards. As our passengers depart into Paris, there are already large numbers gathering in Eurostar's mezzanine departures lounge having checked in for the next train to Waterloo.

Left: TMST No 3206 awaits departure from Paris Gare du Nord on a pre-commissioning run on 2 July 1994. *Colin J. Marsden*

From Lille to Brussels

We pick up train No 9116 at Lille. This service departed from Waterloo International at 08.27 and was also scheduled to call at Ashford International (at 09.27) before arrival at Lille at 11.30. In fact on this particular occasion the train arrived three minutes late at 11.33. In an adjacent platform is one of the TGV units, No 4507. With the doors once again closed, we are ready to depart and the driver eases the controller forward to accelerate away at 11.36.34. The train passes under the Lille-Roubaix line before veering across sharply to the right to join the traditional SNCF route out of Lille towards Valenciennes. Until the completion of the high-speed line through Belgium — which will diverge from the LGV-Nord at Fretin — Eurostar services have to use the normal tracks through Belgium. The line linking Lille with Froyennes opened on 1 December 1865 and the Lille-Tournai line was electrified from 25 May 1993.

Having passed onto the traditional route, the train heads east passing over the LGV-Nord line before reaching Lezennes (11.40.10). Alongside the tracks are storage sidings of SNCF occupied by spare TGV sets awaiting their next duty and by two Class 25xxx locomotives. On the left is SNCF's Hellemmes Works and as we press on eastwards an SNCB Class 12 electric locomotive, No 1209, one of a batch of introduced in 1986, heads westwards. These locomotives, capable of operating on both 25kV dc and 3,000V ac, are designed for use on the Antwerp-Mouscron-Lille route. Hellemmes station is followed by those at Pont-de-Bois, Annappes (11.42.08) and Ascq (11.42.35). Immediately after Ascq, the single-track, non-electrified branch to Orchies heads south; at this point the new high-speed line is still to the south.

We are now approaching Baisieux, the last station in France, which is passed at 11.45.20. Crossing the Belgian border, the only immediate change is that the lineside equipment is Belgian rather than French, and that the kilometre posts now record the distances from Brussels. It is over the section from Baisieux to Froyennes that our driver has to make his last switch of power supply; this time from the 25kV of France to the 3,000V dc of Belgium. Again this change is achieved with consummate skill, so that the travelling passengers notice little, other than a slight brake application on the approaches to the junction at Froyennes where the line from Mouscron comes in from the northwest. The junction and Froyennes station are safely negotiated. Tournai station is passed at 11.52.55; in the station is SNCF No 67605 with a westbound train. Stabled in the sidings is SNCB two-car unit No 431, one of 140 similar units delivered from BN between 1980 and 1984. As our train passes through

Left: In August 1996 a London-bound Eurostar passes through Ath station headed by No 3216. *Alan F. Reekie*

Below left: A Brussels-bound Eurostar passes a Brussels-Tournai push-pull train at the temporary station at Halle in October 1995. Evidence of the construction of the new Belgian high-speed line is visible in the foreground. *Alan F. Reekie*

Above right: A London-bound Eurostar crosses to Line 94 south of Halle station using temporary trackwork in March 1996. *Alan F. Reekie*

Right: A Brussels-London Eurostar service passes through temporary track 3 at Halle station in April 1996. *Alan F. Reekie*

Below: Having passed through Halle, a Brussels-bound Eurostar heads northbound alongside the early work of the Belgian high-speed line in October 1995. *Alan F. Reekie*

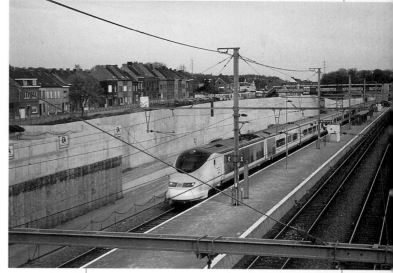

Tournai a second EMU, No 418, departs with a southbound train; this will take the line towards Basècles-Carrières.

The station through which the Eurostar service has just passed dates from 1879. The line from Mouscron via Froyennes to Tournai — the first to serve the town — opened in 1842 and the current station was the third station to be constructed and postdates the opening of the line to Maffles (1854) and that to Basècles (1870). A line built in 1875 linked the new station site with the route towards Maffles and it is over this route that our train now departs. Immediately to the south of Tournai is a huge rail-served industrial site and it is at this point that the Basècles and Maffles routes diverge. We continue to head east over SNCB route No 94. We are now heading towards Leuze, 16km away, where in 1885 the redundant building from one of Tournai's earlier stations was reconstructed to serve. As we head east a westbound passenger train heads back towards Tournai.

The maximum speed on the section of track towards Leuze is 140km and as we approach the town, the trackbed of the now closed route south towards Basècles comes in from the right. Leuze is passed at 12.02.13, after a slight brake application on the approach to the station, and immediately after the station a single-track non-electrified line heads north; this is the line towards Ronse (Renaix) — SNCB route No 86 — which remains operational, albeit disused.

From Leuze to Ath (Aat), the distance is some 10km, which our train completes in some six minutes. Immediately before Ath station there is the junction with the line

Above: Pictured shortly before the Belgian high-speed line opened, a London-bound Eurostar approaches Halle from the north in October 1997. *Alan F. Reekie*

from Geraardsbergen (Grammont) and Ghent — SNCB route No 91 which has recently been electrified — which comes in from the left. As we pass over the junction at 12.08.22 an SNCB train from the north is held at the signals; it will follow us into Ath. Our train rushes through Ath station at 12.08.37; on the adjacent platform No 3 SNCB EMU No 176, one of 120 two-car units built between 1962 and 1965, awaits departure. One curious fact that will be unknown to most passengers on the train is that both the 51 and 52km posts are passed quickly whilst travelling through the station; this is a reflection that the current route used, via Halle, is one kilometre shorter than the original route via Ghislenghien.

On the east side of Ath station the lines divide. The original route now terminates at Ghislenghien as a freight only route serving a Citroën site. Our train takes the middle route towards Halle, whilst the third line heads southeastwards towards Maffles. As we continue to follow SNCB route No 94, we pass a westbound Eurostar service at 12.09.40; this is the 12.31 departure from Brussels-Midi — train No 9133 — which is due to arrive in London at 14.43. For a short distance after departing from Ath we head eastwards, before we curve round to head northeastwards to Brussels. It is at this point that we can see to our right the evidence of the construction of the Belgian high-speed link and at km post 46 there is a connection from our line to give access to the construction work. With the construction work proceeding apace alongside, we pass through Silly (Opzullik) station at 12.14.45. Some 5km further on the high-speed line diverges, taking a more

southerly route to avoid the town of Enghien (Edingen).

As we approach Enghien there is a brief brake application to reduce our speed to 90km/h for the junction with the line northwards to Geraardsbergen (SNCB route No 123), which we pass at 12.19.04 and the station at Enghien follows some 16sec later. Enghien was also the junction of the line towards Braine-le-Comte, but this has now been dismantled following a period out of use. As we continue to head eastwards we are passed by two trains — a westbound passenger service and an SNCB light engine — both heading towards Enghien. Initially the line towards Mons heads northeastwards with a gentle curvature, but as we approach Mons, there is a sharp curve to the east, which requires three brief brake applications and as we decelerate towards the junction, a further westbound passenger train passes us.

Shortly before Halle, the two tracks from Ath join the two tracks of the existing main line from Paris to Brussels. This junction will be significantly modified with the completion of the high-speed line and there is considerable evidence of the new work. The track plan, both before and after the completion of the new route, is shown in the adjacent line drawing (see page 96).

The junction at Halle is approached over a sharp set of reverse curves, which require the driver to make two brake applications before the junction is traversed at some 40km/h. As we join the Brussels-Jurbise line, a southbound passenger service passes.

Above left: With construction work for the new high-speed line proceeding in the foreground, the 12.31 Eurostar service from Brussels-Midi to Waterloo International heads past Lot on 1 June 1995. *Paul Shannon*

Left: During the summer of 1997, the rear of a Brussels-bound Eurostar service passes the new viaduct at Lot under construction as part of the improvements between Halle and Brussels. *Alan F. Reekie*

The junction at Halle, 13km from Brussels-Midi, is passed at 12.28.43. At the time of writing, Halle station is still provided with four platforms on the surface; with the completion of the high-speed line it will be relocated underground and see the number of platforms increase to six. Our train passes through platform No 1 at 12.29.40; in one of the adjacent platforms is SNCB unit No 827, one of a batch of 44 four-car EMUs built between 1975 and 1979. Immediately to the north of Halle the existing four tracks become three, with a bidirectional line providing access, via Buizingen Junction, to the electrified route towards Beersel that runs to the east of Brussels. To the east the new track and catenary indicate the alignment of the new high-speed line.

Having traversed Buizingen Junction, our train passes through Buizingen station (12.31.55) before a slight brake application on the approach to Lot. A two-car EMU, No 615, heads southbound. We pass through platform No 3 at Lot at 12.35.20 after which there is a slight brake application. Ruisbroek station is passed at 12.35.34; to the north of the station a new flyover is under construction. This will provide a connection with the electrified freight-only line that runs to the west of Brussels to Jette in place of the existing ladder junction (see diagram). Forest-Midi is passed at 12.38.15. Immediately after the station, to the west of the train, is situated the SNCB depot at Forest; this is home both to the Belgian TMSTs and also the Brussels base for the Thalys TGVs on the services between Amsterdam, Rotterdam, Brussels and Paris.

Forest depot is a purpose-built facility constructed on the site of an earlier SNCB EMU depot. The stock from the original depot was transferred away in October 1990 to allow the new depot to be built. It is planned that Forest will have the capacity to deal with five TMST rakes per night.

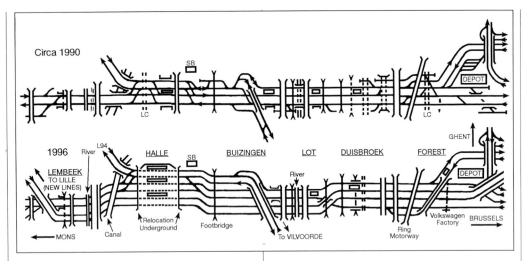

Circa 1990

1996

GHENT

LEMBEEK
TO LILLE
(NEW LINES)

L94
River

HALLE   SB   BUIZINGEN   LOT   DUISBROEK   FOREST

River

DEPOT

MONS

Canal

Relocation
Underground

Footbridge

To VILVOORDE

Ring
Motorway

Volkswagen
Factory

BRUSSELS

SB

LC

LC

DEPOT

Immediately to the north of Forest depot we pass under the Forest East-Jette line; to the right, heading towards Forest East, can be seen two two-car EMUs, Nos 382 and 377; these thyristor controlled units were built between 1980 and 1984. A third of the type, No 339, heads southbound toward Lot as we approach Brussels-Midi. As we decelerate towards our destination, a rake of SNCF coaches is taken as ECS towards Forest depot headed by SNCB No 2751; this is one of 60 Class 27 Bo-Bo electric locomotives built between 1981 and 1983. On the approaches to Brussels-Midi a large number of units are visible,

Above: The inter-relationship between the old and the new routes from Halle to Forest in Belgium. The Volkswagen works at Forest is the location of the new siding illustrated in the following photographs.

Below: The rear of a northbound Eurostar heads towards Brussels at the junction of Line 96 with Line 26 at Buizingen in December 1997. *Alan F. Reekie*

Above right: With construction work again visible, a Brussels-bound Eurostar heads northbound at Ruisbroek during March 1997. *Alan F. Reekie*

Below right: Running along Line 96, with the new high-speed lines in the centre, a Brussels-bound Eurostar service heads north at Ruisbroek during the summer of 1997. *Alan F. Reekie*

stabled awaiting their next duties. These include two-car units No 258, built in the early 1960s, and No 687, built a decade later. Also visible is SNCB shunter No 8002, the second of the diesel-hydraulic Class 80 0-6-0 shunters introduced in 1960. As we pull into the Brussels-Midi Eurostar platforms, another Class 27 electric locomotive, No 2733, departs from the main station with a southbound service.

Work started on the construction of the Eurostar terminal at Brussels-Midi in October 1992. Eventually the station will have six international platforms. Two will be for the use of Eurostar services, a third will be used by TGV services, whilst the remaining three will be used by the Thalys trains linking Amsterdam and Rotterdam with Paris.

The Eurostar platforms at Brussels-Midi are segregated from the remainder of the station; unlike the other two partners in the Eurostar consortium, Belgium alone has retained passport control in the terminal building, along with the customs hall. With the arrival at 12.44, the passengers gather together their luggage and disembark, making their way to the escalators that lead to passport control. Another 'Three Capitals' service has been safely completed.

Below: With the 'Canal du Charleroi' in the background, a Brussels-bound Eurostar heads northbound, away from the camera, towards its destination in June 1997. *Alan F. Reekie*

Inset: The rear of a London-bound Eurostar runs 'wrong line' past track re-laying near Forest in August 1997. *Alan F. Reekie*

Above left: In May 1997, a Brussels-bound Eurostar passes the site of the new Line 96A viaduct at Forest-Midi. This view, looking north, shows the train heading away from the camera. *Alan F. Reekie*

Left: A London-bound Eurostar heads south towards the camera past the construction work for the new viaduct at Forest-Midi in June 1997. It is interesting to note the difference between this and the previous illustration in terms of the actual construction work. *Alan F. Reekie*

Above: Six months later and the new viaduct at Forest-Midi is complete. A London-bound Eurostar approaches the station at Forest-Midi from the north running '*contre-voie*' ('wrong line'). *Alan F. Reekie*

Right: With work in the foreground on a new transfer siding for Volkswagen, a Brussels-bound Eurostar heads towards its destination at Forest in May 1997. *Alan F. Reekie*

Above: A service from Brussels-Midi to Waterloo International passes the site of the new Volkswagen transfer siding in August 1997. *Alan F. Reekie*

Left: Pictured at Forest depot in March 1997, this Eurostar power car suffered front-end damage at a foggy level crossing. The damage allows for a close view of the Scharfenburg coupling with which these units are fitted. These are normally well-hidden from public view. *Alan F. Reekie*

Above right: A Brussels-bound Eurostar service passes Forest-Midi on route L96A heading towards its destination in May 1997. *Alan F. Reekie*

Right: The 10.23 Eurostar service from Waterloo is pictured after arrival at Brussels-Midi station on 25 October 1994. Set No 3003 is nearest the camera, with No 3004 completing the train. *Brian Morrison*

Above: A London-bound Eurostar, headed by No 3106, awaits its departure signal at Brussels-Midi in March 1996. This is one of the eight rakes allocated to Forest depot. *Alan F. Reekie*

Left: As the evening sun catches the front of TMST set No 3228 at Brussels-Midi on 12 August 1995, passengers gather for a trip back to London Waterloo. Few of the passengers who make the trip will be aware of the complexity of the train upon which they are about to travel or of the nature of the operation behind it; they will be happy that, with the completion of the Channel Tunnel, it is now possible to travel speedily by rail between Europe and Britain. *Author*

Via the Catford Loop

A s already mentioned, there are occasions when Eurostar services are routed via the alternative Catford Loop. This line is designated CTR2 and is common with the main CTR1 as far as Brixton Junction. At this point, as already recounted, CTR1 heads through Brixton station and on towards Penge. CTR2 heads almost due east at this point towards Denmark Hill.

On this occasion we are onboard the 08.27 service (train No 9116) from London Waterloo to Brussels-Midi. Departure from Waterloo is on time, which means that we reach Brixton Junction just before 08.37. After a mile we pass through Canterbury Road Junction, where a double-track connection leads down to the route into Blackfriars and the Thameslink route. We cross over these lines before a second connection comes in at Cambria Junction. Passing through the short Denmark Hill Tunnel (63yd in length) we trundle through platform 4 at Denmark Hill station (at 08.39.05) on the down Catford Loop line. As we enter Grove Tunnel (132yd) an adverse signal forces us to decelerate slightly as an inbound 12-car EMU heads towards London; unit No 3802 brings up the rear. Peckham Rye station follows (at 08.40.15) after which the line into London Bridge dives underneath; our train is now on the double-track section towards Nunhead. The single island platform at

Nunhead is passed at 08.41.25; immediately after the station our driver applies the brakes so that he can negotiate Nunhead Junction and take the line southeastwards towards Shortlands.

As we pass through the junction a rake of EMUs, formed of Classes 465 and 466, head inbound, carrying their load of commuters towards London. Half a mile further on we cross over the four-track main line from Norwood Junction towards London Bridge. Crofton Park station is passed at 08.43.30; again we are faced by adverse signals which require our driver to brake twice between Crofton Park and the next station, Catford, which is passed at 08.44.45. After Catford the train swings to a more easterly direction and passes over the Addiscombe branch. Bellingham is passed at 08.46; at this time in the morning the three carriage sidings situated to the east on the down side are empty. Passing through the station our driver accelerates to counter the up gradient at this point before passing through Beckenham Hill station at 08.46.45. The final station on the Catford Loop is Ravensbourne, which we trundle through at 08.48. We finally meet up with the main CTR1 again at Shortlands Junction at 08.48.45.

It is interesting to note that the journey time over the Catford Loop route, at just under 12min, is only fractionally longer than that via the main route.

Above left: Diverted over the Catford Loop because of engineers' possession of the main route, the 10.19 Paris Gare du Nord-Waterloo International service approaches Catford on 2 July 1995. The train is formed of sets Nos 3008 (leading) and 3007. *Brian Morrison*

Left: On 2 July 1995, the 12.14 Waterloo-Brussels service passes through Catford. The train is formed of TMST sets Nos 3213 (leading) and 3214, one of the French-allocated sets. *Brian Morrison*

Above: The 12.14 service from Waterloo to Brussels, diverted via the Catford Loop, passes Beckenham Hill on 24 March 1996. The train was formed of TMST sets Nos 3223 (leading) and 3224. *Brian Morrison*

A diverted Eurostar service — the 11.52 from Waterloo to Paris formed of TMST sets Nos 3229 and 3230 — passes Ravensbourne station on the Catford Loop on 14 January 1996. *Brian Morrison*

The Route via Maidstone

In order to provide a diversionary route from Bickley to Ashford, the line from Bickley Junction through St Mary Cray, Swanley, Maidstone East and Charing is also cleared for the operation of Eurostar trains. This route is some 46 miles in length as opposed to some 43 by the main route. The line is also more heavily graded, with a maximum of 1 in 60 for 1.5 miles between Maidstone East and Bearsted.

Ironically, the proposed Channel Tunnel Rail Link will run parallel to this route, to a point between Bearsted and Hollingbourne where it will take a more northerly alignment.

Below: The diverted 14.10 Waterloo International-Brussels Midi passes Bearsted station on 20 October 1996 with No 3213 leading No 3214. *Brian Morrison*

Left: formed of TMST Nos 3107 (at the front) and 3108 bringing up the rear, the diverted 11.31 Brussels-Midi-Waterloo International passes near Hollingbourne on 20 October 1996. *Brian Morrison*

Right: The diverted 11.43 Waterloo-Paris service passes Lenham on 20 October 1996 formed of Nos 3207 (leading) and 3208. The Class 423/1 '4VEP' No 3588, which was forming the 10.20 Victoria-Ashford International service had been routed into the loop to allow for the passage of the Eurostar. Until the completion of the high-speed line from London to the Channel Tunnel, Eurostar trains will always have to compete with domestic services for scarce paths. *Brian Morrison*

Below: The sleek lines of the Eurostar train, formed of Nos 3207 and 3208, look slightly incongruous amidst the detritus found alongside so many railway lines as it forms the 11.43 service from Waterloo to Paris on 20 October 1996. The train is seen approaching Lenham station. *Brian Morrison*

Bottom right: Gradient profile of the route between Swanley and Ashford.

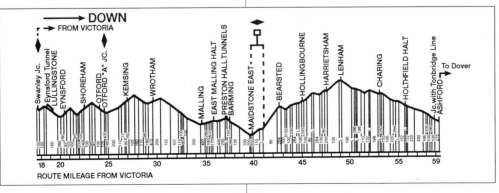

Above: Pictured climbing between Lenham and Charing, this dramatic view of the 09.14 Waterloo-Brussels Eurostar service, formed of Nos 3229 (leading) and 3230, on 20 October 1996 shows the undulating nature of the route to good advantage. *Brian Morrison*

Below: A final view covering the diversionary route via Maidstone sees the 08.10 Waterloo-Paris service sweeping round the curve between Charing and Hothfield on 20 October 1996. The train is formed of Nos 3002 (leading) and 3001. *Brian Morrison*